NO LONGER PROPERTY OF
SEATTLE PUBLIC LIBRARY

YOUNG WORLD RISING

YOUNG WORLD RISING

How Youth, Technology and Entrepreneurship are Changing the World from the Bottom Up

ROB SALKOWITZ

WILEY

John Wiley & Sons, Inc.

Copyright © 2010 by Rob Salkowitz. All rights reserved.

Published by John Wiley & Sons, Inc., Hoboken, New Jersey.
Published simultaneously in Canada.

No part of this publication may be reproduced, stored in a retrieval system, or transmitted in any form or by any means, electronic, mechanical, photocopying, recording, scanning, or otherwise, except as permitted under Section 107 or 108 of the 1976 United States Copyright Act, without either the prior written permission of the publisher, or authorization through payment of the appropriate per-copy fee to the Copyright Clearance Center, Inc., 222 Rosewood Drive, Danvers, MA 01923, (978) 750-8400, fax (978) 646-8600, or on the web at www.copyright.com. Requests to the publisher for permission should be addressed to the Permissions Department, John Wiley & Sons, Inc., 111 River Street, Hoboken, NJ 07030, (201) 748-6011, via fax at (201) 748-6008, or online at www.wiley.com/go/permissions.

Limit of Liability/Disclaimer of Warranty: While the publisher and author have used their best efforts in preparing this book, they make no representations or warranties with respect to the accuracy or completeness of the contents of this book and specifically disclaim any implied warranties of merchantability or fitness for a particular purpose. No warranty may be created or extended by sales representatives or written sales materials. The advice and strategies contained herein may not be suitable for your situation. You should consult with a professional where appropriate. Neither the publisher nor author shall be liable for any loss of profit or any other commercial damages, including but not limited to special, incidental, consequential, or other damages.

For general information on our other products and services or for technical support, please contact our Customer Care Department within the United States at (800) 762-2974, outside the United States at (317) 572-3993, or via fax at (317) 572-4002.

Wiley also publishes its books in a variety of electronic formats. Some content that appears in print may not be available in electronic books. For more information about Wiley products, visit our web site at www.wiley.com.

Library of Congress Cataloging-in-Publication Data

Salkowitz, Rob, 1967-
    Young world rising : how youth technology and entrepreneurship are changing the world from the bottom up / Rob Salkowitz.
        p. cm. — (Microsoft executive leadership series)
    Includes bibliographical references and index.
    ISBN 978-0-470-41780-5 (cloth)
        1. Technology and youth—Developing countries.   2. Information technology—Developing countries.   3. Computer networks—Developing countries.   4. Generation Y—Developing countries.   I. Title.
    T14.5.S223 2010
    303.48'3091724—dc22

                                                                         2010004442

Printed in the United States of America
10 9 8 7 6 5 4 3 2 1

ABOUT THE EXECUTIVE LEADERSHIP SERIES

The Microsoft Executive Leadership Series is pleased to present independent perspectives from some of today's leading thinkers on the ways that IT innovations are transforming how organizations operate and how people work. The role of information technology in business, society, and our lives continues to increase, creating new challenges and opportunities for organizations of all types. The titles in this series are aimed at business leaders, policy-makers, and anyone interested in the larger strategic questions that arise from the convergence of people, communication media, business process, and software.

Microsoft is supporting this series to promote richer discussions around technology and business issues. We hope that each title in the series contributes to a greater understanding of the complex uncertainties facing organizations operating in a fast-changing and deeply connected new world of work, and is useful in the internal dialogues that every business conducts as it plans for the future. It remains our privilege and our commitment to be part of those conversations.

CONTENTS

PREFACE

This book began with a question.

It was at one of the keynote presentations I was doing around the material in my first book, *Generation Blend: Managing Across the Technology Age Gap*, which talked about how generational differences could complicate the efforts of organizations to implement "Web 2.0" social computing technologies and engage the cohort of workers who grew up marinated in digital culture. The questioner asked, in accented English, whether the differences and the strategies I talked about would apply in countries where the demographics were "upside down"—that is, where young people vastly outnumbered their elders. I said I wasn't sure, but I could do some research.

Two years later, here is the product of that research.

It's not the book I imagined. In fact, if I'd imagined this book from the start, I doubt I would have had the audacity to attempt it. Instead, I was led into this project by trying to explore a more narrow subject: the similarities and differences in the attitudes of the Net Generation in developed and emerging economies, and how these might be shaping the future of work.

Needless to say, the entire subject of information and communication technology (ICT) in emerging technologies is rather complex. Fortunately, I was engaged by one of my corporate clients to undertake research along these lines. I had a large amount of data at my disposal and a corps of experts and analysts to help me interpret it.

That project allowed me to recognize the trend at the center of *Young World Rising,* one of the most exciting developments in recent economic history: the emergence of a new global ethos of entrepreneurship, seeded by massive investments in capacity-building by governments, non-government organizations (NGOs), and multinationals, fueled by the spread of networks and connectivity, and fired by the burgeoning ambitions of a global generation of young people more than 4 billion strong.

The scale and importance of that story seemed to dwarf any tactical insights I might have discovered about the behaviors of Net Generation workers within existing organizations. Across what I came to call the Young World, the next generation is not waiting for opportunities to arrive or for institutions to keep decades-old promises. They are making their own futures. And, incidentally, they are making all of ours as well.

As I began reaching out to young entrepreneurs all around the world, talking to experts, combing through books, papers and Web sites, I began to perceive some important commonalities in the approaches taken by startups (specifically, software and services companies, who are able to leverage networks and knowledge to create new wealth from very modest capital) across the Young World, regardless of size, scope, or location.

The Millennial generation in the Old World makes its presence felt by transforming existing institutions—the workplace, civil society, the consumer marketplace—with its new norms and approaches. The rising generation in the Young World is marshalling significant resources to create new models to replace the dilapidated and dysfunctional legacies that previously defined their environments. For these young entrepreneurs, it is not just about the success of their own business, but about creating a better model for *all* business: one that is appropriate for a resource-constrained world and that attempts to compensate for arbitrary boundaries that globalization and networks now render obsolete. Their new organizations have Net Generation values woven into their DNA, and have enormous transformative potential as they spread and grow.

In both the Old and Young Worlds, the challenge for incumbent institutions is to find ways to blend the vast potential of Net Generation approaches with the wisdom and knowledge of mature experience. Finding ways to achieve that blend is what motivated my earlier work on the digital age divide in the Old World knowledge workforce, and it is what drives me to explore the issues of the Net Generation in a global perspective.

During this project, I was fortunate to make the acquaintance of scores of experts and professionals in the fields of economics, international development, international business, technology, and demographics who were kind enough to share some of their insights with me. My goal was to synthesize these very specific fields of expertise into a broader view that would be actionable by business leaders, policymakers, and others whose success depends on understanding larger trends going on in the world as they plan future strategy.

The discussions with the experts were enlightening, but my favorite conversations were with the young entrepreneurs. I am an entrepreneur myself, having participated in the creation of seven companies since 1994 (when I was 25), including the digital communications firm in Seattle where I remain a principal. The mindset and the experiences of the young innovators I spoke to resonate strongly with me, as does their idealism. It was my privilege to give them voice in this forum.

So this is where a simple question can lead. I didn't know that it would take me, 14 months later, to a modest home off the busy streets of Bangalore, India to sit and have tea with the youngest member of the World Economic Forum (and his mother), or that I would end up lobbing a boulder into the pond instead of a pebble.

I don't expect my analysis to meet with universal agreement, or the insights of the entrepreneurs profiled in these pages to be treated as gospel. At best, both are food for thought. Will the Young World rise? Outcomes are never certain, but after hearing these stories, perhaps there is reason to hope.

Rob Salkowitz
Seattle, Washington
June 2010

YOUNG WORLD RISING

INTRODUCTION

Suhas Gopinath knew he was in trouble. He had failed an exam at his high school in Bangalore, and his mother would not be happy. Like middle-class mothers the world over, she believed strongly in education as the means to achieve a good life and a stable job, and leaned hard on her children to excel at school. Surely she would take his poor result on the exam as proof that something was amiss with the extracurricular activity that was taking up more and more of his waking hours.

"You are spending too much time at that Internet café," she said to her 15-year-old son. "You must swear on my head that you won't visit that shop and will focus on your studies!"

"But mother, what about Bill Gates?" replied Suhas.

"What about him?"

"He's the richest man in the world, a great entrepreneur who built his company from scratch, and he never finished his studies, so why do you force me to?"

Bill Gates, who has spent a considerable portion of his fortune promoting education around the world, would probably not approve of young Suhas's reasoning, but he might allow himself a certain pride in the achievements of the young man he inspired.

The reason Suhas was failing in his studies is that he was spending his nights building Web sites for businesses in the United States, a skill he taught himself at age 14 when he minded the local cyber café during the owner's daily lunch break. Seeing the boy's talent, the owner suggested he register as a freelance developer.

For the first year, it was tough going. Suhas did not have a PC at home and had to work at the Internet shop. A friend in the United States helped him generate sales leads, but companies were reluctant to do business with someone so young and lacking in formal academic credentials.

Suhas eventually hit on a strategy to reach his target market of small manufacturers. He would identify prospects from the phone listings, seeking out companies that had e-mail addresses but no Web presence. He sent the companies e-mail inquiries suggesting that he represented a firm in India interested in placing a large order for import. The companies would respond to the opportunity, offering to mail out printed catalogs because they were not on the Web. Suhas then curtly informed them that he could not do business with them, because their lack of e-commerce capabilities did not meet his supply standards. Several weeks later, he followed up with a brochure from his real company, Globals Inc., offering to design and develop a site at an attractive price.

This scheme was such a success that it is now studied in marketing programs at Indian business schools. "I am sure that none of those companies regret their decisions," said Suhas. "They are small businesses in a global economy and they need to be on the Web, for themselves and their customers. The next inquiry they receive might be real."

Suhas spent the remainder of his teenage years building up his company. The first employee he hired nearly turned down the job offer when he found out his boss was only 15. Suhas reassured him that he was not interested in strict hierarchies in his company and everyone would be treated as colleagues. He stuck to that approach as the business scaled up from building five sites per month to fifty.

Over the next several years, Globals grew to employ 120 people in 12 locations worldwide, but the company culture is still rooted in that same ethic, where team members are given respect and room to express their talent. On Friday afternoons, visitors might find the

Bangalore offices dark, and the team of hardened IT professionals—most in their mid-20s—blowing off steam playing hide and seek with their 21-year-old CEO.

Suhas tried to keep up with his studies, but his attendance problems at the local university were so severe that the school would not allow him to sit for his final exams. In this case, however, the truant had a unique excuse. "I had joined the World Economic Forum and was traveling quite a bit," Suhas explained. Indeed, the international organization, whose annual meetings in Davos, Switzerland feature a who's-who of the global elite from Bill Clinton to Nandan Nilekani, honored Suhas Gopinath, its youngest member, as Young Entrepreneur of the Year in 2008.

One of Suhas's professors, recognizing the innovator's dilemma of having to balance school work with the responsibilities of a global executive, summoned him to the faculty chambers to offer a compromise: He'd ignore his student's abysmal attendance record, but was interested in seeking other employment. Perhaps Suhas would consider his application to work at Globals?

Today, Suhas presides over an expanding IT services business that is experiencing strong growth amid the global recession by helping its clients save the costs of developing their applications and managing their data centers. He is a passionate advocate for entrepreneurism, meeting with everyone from students to government leaders to promote the virtues of forging one's own destiny in a society where most educated young people still prefer the predictability of a paycheck from the government or a large company.

Despite the influence of his example and his energy, there are still people who remain to be convinced. His mother, who once scolded him for failing a high school exam, still frets that his unsettled lifestyle will make it hard for him to find a bride, and sometimes asks if it would be possible for him to put one of his friends in charge of Globals so he could go and get a steady job working for Infosys.

* * *

Suhas Gopinath has received a lot of attention in the global media. Who can resist the story of the teenaged CEO sipping champagne with the grandees of Davos when he's barely of legal age to buy a beer at the corner shop? Some might say his case is exceptional: In a country of more than a billion people, it is possible to stumble upon a one-in-a-billion individual.

The sheer novelty of Suhas's personal story should not obscure the larger point. This ambitious young man found success because of his talent, to be sure. But he also benefited from a unique confluence of powerful forces that is extending the opportunity to express talent more broadly across the globe and more deeply into the socioeconomic scale with each passing day.

The spread of information networks and the development of information and communication technology (ICT) skills across a broader swath of the workforce open new avenues to prosperity that did not exist even a decade ago in many parts of the world. It also creates a whole new set of opportunities and uncertainties for global businesses. The old problems of the Young World may still remain, but the introduction of this new dynamic can begin to bend the curve upward.

Young World Rising traces the shape of that bending curve.

A BRIGHT AND CROWDED FUTURE

As we look ahead to the second decade of the 21st century, the global economy is at a crossroads. Industrial-age institutions have reached their breaking point, and it is not clear whether the frantic efforts of the established order will bring about their renewal or just drag out the process of collapse. Even if recovery from the 2008 financial crisis happens quickly, what character will it assume? Will leadership come from the top, or from the bottom? Will change be driven by reform at the center, or by insurgency from the edge?

The answers to those questions have enormous consequences for organizations that have to plan ahead. Every company wants to stay out in front of changes in its industry and markets. Every company wants a clear roadmap. But the road ahead is far from clear. A world in which change and innovation come from outside the traditional channels presents a far different set of challenges from one in which large, archaic institutions cling to power and extract subsidies from governments terrified to let them fail. Either future is possible, but which one do you plan for?

Given the stakes, firms need to cover their bets by considering a range of possible futures, not just the ones that seem most likely or convenient from the present vantage point.[1]

Young World Rising spells out one direction forward, working through the implications of a world in which growth and innovation are driven by young countries, new workstyles, networked organizational structures, and business models enabled by the borderless spread of knowledge and talent. It is meant to help organizations develop a strategy to reach new markets, engage new talent, anticipate new sources of competition, and think through the changes they need to make to adapt.

Young World Rising is not a prediction. It's a rich description of, and argument for, a future scenario in which the world looks very different from the one many of us might expect. Nonetheless, this future may come about if several forces combine in ways that, in retrospect, would appear entirely inevitable and unsurprising. It may be taking shape before our eyes, though we are too distracted by other issues to see it. If the dynamics driving the rise of the Young World are not derailed by other uncertainties, businesses and organizations will need to pivot their management practices and technology investments to adapt. But first, they will need to understand the forces at work and appreciate the motivations driving the change.

Typically, conversations about global economic change in the 21st century are dominated by questions about the role of China. Those questions are important, but *Young World Rising* is not a story about China.* Though China is an enormous, rapidly (but unevenly) developing country with vast potential, it, and Russia, and most of Eastern Europe, remain closer to the West and Japan in terms of demographics. China also sits apart from most of the world in terms of the ability of its government to drive both economic development and social regimentation (see "What About China?").

---

*One big problem is that the catchy acronym BRIC (Brazil–Russia–India–China) has become shorthand for a certain view of emerging markets, and encourages businesses to see these very different countries as in some way similar. If demographics and market-based entrepreneurship are key determinants, then China and Russia have little place in a discussion of the Young World, whereas India and Brazil are central to it.

WHAT ABOUT CHINA?

When it comes to discussions of emerging economies, China is the 900-pound panda in the room. The growth of China is undoubtedly the biggest economic story of the half-century 1980–2030. Though its core regions are now fully modernized, parts of China, home to hundreds of millions of people, still bear close resemblance to less-developed countries, and face many of the same challenges. Over the next 20–30 years, it is highly likely that China as a whole will experience the same sort of escalation in living standards as a result of technology and indigenous business creation. However, there are a few reasons why China doesn't fit in with a discussion of youth, social technology, and entrepreneurship in emerging economies.

1. *China is not young*. China's working age population will peak in 2016 and then diminish for the rest of the century. Goldman Sachs projects that China's median age will rise from 33 in 2005 to 45 in 2050, while India's, for example, will continue to hold steady at around 26. By 2030, China may have as many senior citizens 65 and over as children under 15.[2] Those are Old World demographics, not Young World ones.
2. *China is not open to social technology*. China has one of the highest levels of Internet and mobile penetration of any country in the world. However, the government maintains almost obsessive control over access to information, using filtering technologies and heavy-handed censorship to limit the subject matter that its citizens can access and discuss. It is profoundly uncertain whether innovation can flourish under these conditions, given the kinds of open, freewheeling collaborative conversations that go on elsewhere in the world.
3. *China is enterprising, not entrepreneurial*. "In China, the government is the entrepreneur," writes Harvard Business School professor Tarun Khanna.[3] That is, entrepreneurship is government-led and financed primarily through extremely opaque transactions with government-run banks. Its highly-productive economy retains many vestiges of state control and central planning, indicating a top-down rather than bottom-up development model.

4. *China is not "emerging."* It has emerged. By 2020, it will be the world's second largest economy behind the United States.

China has methods at its disposal to solve its problems; these methods are unique to its scale, its society, and its political system but are not practical or desirable as models across the Young World. There are plenty of great sources of insight on the implications and strategies surrounding China's rise. *Young World Rising* is primarily focused on developments elsewhere in the world.

Rather than looking to the Silk Road as the path to the future, *Young World Rising* makes the case for an entirely different and less-expected direction forward: a world in which new growth and innovation comes from outside the established centers of the global economy (including China), and from the bottom up. The optimism, energy, and entrepreneurial spirit of youth are channeled through the medium of information networks, driving sustainable growth by creating new markets and better solutions to local and global problems. It's a world where the arbitrary dictates of geography and history do not limit the potential of talented, ambitious young people to make a difference, solve a problem, reach an audience, find dignified employment, or create opportunities for others.

Suhas Gopinath may be an extraordinary example of that dynamic, but he is far from the only one. As we will see, the spirit of entrepreneurship and the power of information networks are spreading rapidly across the globe, carrying the seeds of economic renewal. The diffusion of knowledge and skills changes the landscape for businesses, governments, labor markets, and consumers. Demographic patterns suggest that these forces will have greater impact in those parts of the world where youth and young thinking predominate—which is to say, today's emerging markets and less developed countries. As emerging markets emerge, they will increasingly influence affairs in the old centers of the 20th century world, profoundly reordering the geo-economic landscape, and potentially the geopolitical one as well.

Some might object that this is a brighter vision of the future than conditions warrant. By mid-century, the global population is projected to peak somewhere in the neighborhood of 9.7 billion (compared to 6.8 billion in 2010), and it is possible to imagine scenarios of Malthusian horror as an overcrowded planet is stripped bare of resources and decimated by conflict. At the very least, we are conditioned to view with alarm the idea of all those *billions of mouths to feed*, in parts of the world that already bear crushing burdens of poverty and underdevelopment.

The picture of the future painted in *Young World Rising* does not ignore the reality of those billions of mouths to feed, but rather suggests the possibility that billions of minds working together and billions of hands pulling in the same direction might be able to stay a step ahead of the challenges of scarcity and sustainability. To meet unprecedented challenges, we are able to marshal unprecedented resources.

This is critical to business, governments, and global organizations, because the rise of the Young World has the potential to fundamentally change the character of global markets and the conventional relationships between the old centers of the world economy and those rising at its rugged frontiers.

In the past, the well-developed infrastructures of the Old World centers of production provided a consistent advantage in scale, knowledge, and innovation. Today, the benefits of scale are mitigated by the power of networks to rapidly mobilize communities that don't require the overhead of organized management. The advantages of established infrastructure are diminished by the need to constantly overhaul aging capital and modernize outdated practices in work and government that have developed significant constituencies over the years. Innovation used to rely on proximity to the centers of knowledge and production, but now technology makes time and distance irrelevant.

Most Young World countries remain burdened by legacies of their own: underdevelopment, political instability, social unrest, and the persistence of attitudes that place artificial limits on the potential of individuals, groups, and society. For the Young World to rise, it must grapple with these challenges. Some countries will fail this first attempt, or at least face significant setbacks that derail hopes of rapid, dramatic improvement. These local uncertainties make it hard to use this framework to forecast the futures of specific markets, even if it were possible to capture all the expertise to make those forecasts in one place. *Young World Rising* is not necessarily the specific future of India, Nigeria, Mexico, or Egypt. It does, however, describe a set of dynamics that anyone interested in those markets should consider in any strategic planning efforts.

What evidence supports the rise of the Young World? For that, we must examine three powerful forces that are reshaping the world of the 21st century, and how people and organizations around the world are harnessing them in amazing and inspiring ways.

THREE FORCES RESHAPING THE WORLD

Three forces are reshaping the world of the 21st century: youth, ICT, and entrepreneurship. Each is powerful on its own, as demonstrated by a wealth of statistics and analyses. Together, they have the potential to fire like the pistons of a high-performance engine, each building on and reinforcing the others' impact and driving the global economy in new directions, at high velocity.

These three forces converge around the concept of the global Net Generation: a worldwide cohort born after 1980,[†] also known as Millennials, that has grown up in tandem with the spread of the Internet and digital media and has been socialized with a unique set of expectations, based in part on the capabilities of the new information environment. Like all young people, the members of the Net Generation want to change the world. Unlike most previous cohorts, they actually have the means at their disposal: overwhelming numbers; unprecedented connectivity and access; a sense of global community that transcends old boundaries; and a recognition that market forces can be the ally rather than then enemy of progressive change.

[†] The concept of the Net Generation was first articulated by Don Tapscott in his 1998 book *Growing Up Digital,* followed up in 2008 with *Grown Up Digital.* Tapscott sets the start-date of the Net Generation in 1977, coincident with the appearance of the first consumer PCs. I use 1981, the demographic marker preferred by Neil Howe and the late William Strauss, whose work discusses the Millennial generation in a social and political context broader than their relationship with technology. In this book, all members of the 1981–2000 cohort are Millennials; those who have been exposed to ICT are also members of the Net Generation. I prefer both terms to the oft-used "Gen Y."

Throughout the past 15 years they have been making their influence felt, first as consumers, then as citizens, and now as workers and entrepreneurs. The Net Generation is the bright face of the Young World, and the economic prospects of youthful countries are intimately tied to how quickly and deeply this entrepreneurial and tech-savvy cohort can have an impact.

In developed economies, the rise of the Net Generation, particularly in the workplace and business world, is necessarily a gradual process. Established organizations must reorient decades or centuries of existing practices and existing investments to accommodate the more transparent, immediate, and globally connected workstyle of the digital natives. The transition in leadership from pre-digital Baby Boomers (b. 1946–1962 in the US) to Millennials will take time, even if it is mediated and facilitated by tech-aware Generation X (b. 1963–1980).[4] Even after Millennials constitute a plurality of the working population (estimated around 2020 in the United States), they will still need to accommodate large numbers of older colleagues, partners, and customers—not to mention the persistent political influence of an aging population demanding services and transfer payments while resisting change to social or political institutions.

Elsewhere in the world, it's a different story. The vast majority of the 4.2 billion global Millennials live in emerging economies and less developed countries (LDCs), where the median age of the population is significantly lower. Consider India's population of more than 1.1 billion; 33% of that population is under the age of 15, with only 7.1% over 60. The numbers are even more dramatic in parts of Africa. Some of this is due to the low average life expectancies in poorer nations and to high mortality rates among mature adults due to infectious diseases, violence, and malnutrition. But what it means in demographic terms is that Millennials outside North America, Europe, and Japan have significantly more potential influence within their societies, and considerably greater prospects to make an immediate economic impact if the required skills and resources are accessible.

For the past 20 years, providing access to ICT skills and the Internet has been a cornerstone of the efforts of governments and nongovernmental organizations (NGOs) around the world to promote workforce development, especially in emerging economies and LDCs. However, in many of those countries, the cost of the equipment and the poor state of the surrounding infrastructure made it difficult for these efforts to spread much beyond a limited core, or to take hold in the larger society.

Now those barriers are falling fast. Though landline broadband connections remain rare and expensive outside the developed world, wireless, satellite-based, and high-speed cellular networks are driving rapid and widespread adoption, even in very poor countries. Mobile phones are ubiquitous and increasingly provide data connectivity as well as voice and short message service (SMS). Internet cafés, government-sponsored community centers, and digital divide–oriented NGOs provide Internet access. Most local businesses and nearly all local affiliates of multinational companies provide high-quality Internet access for their employees. Usage of digital media, video games, social networks, blogs, and voice-over-IP (VoIP) services is as common among urban Millennials in emerging economies as in any other community of young people anywhere in the world.

WHAT IS THE KNOWLEDGE ECONOMY?

The rise of the Young World is intimately tied to the increasing importance of the global knowledge economy. Does that mean everyone will become software developers? Not exactly.

The knowledge economy is the set of industries and jobs that depend on the production, distribution, and consumption of information. This includes the traditional information and communication technology industries—computer hardware, software, consumer electronics, telecommunications, and so on—but it is not limited to them. Entertainment, mass media, professional services, and financial services are all knowledge-economy industries. Industrial-age sectors such as manufacturing, logistics, resource extraction (mining, energy, agriculture), and retail are now permeated with and highly dependent on IT systems and networks for their core operations, and are important customers for knowledge economy services. Most critically, the emerging industries that will likely shape the 21st century economy—biotechnology, nanotechnology, robotics, alternative energy, materials science, and others as-yet undiscovered—will depend on the knowledge and network infrastructures being developed today.

Early exposure to ICT is building skills and capacity among the Young World workforce, but that's only the tip of the iceberg. The transformative effects of mass collaboration at the macro level are just beginning to be understood in the *developed* world, as they flatten hierarchies, expose ideas and organizations to the light of day, and make it ridiculously easy (and cheap) to form communities around common interests. Author and academic Clay Shirky, among others, writes persuasively about how mass collaboration "changes everything" and disrupts the established business models of some of the world's most sophisticated and well-resourced industries.[5]

Now imagine the impact of these technologies in parts of the world where, less than a generation ago, the primary economic activities were agriculture, extractive industries, low-level manufacturing, and bureaucratic government work. All across the Young World, widespread and immediate access to information and global markets has only become mainstream in the past five to ten years, and enormous majorities of the population fit the demographic profile of "early adopters." Change is poised to rip through large swaths of the globe like a brushfire across the savannah.

The important question is *what kind of change*? For that, we should look to a new set of ideas — or perhaps old ideas newly packaged — that are capturing the imagination of policy-makers and opinion leaders focused on economic development, as well as on young populations eager to put the mistakes of the past behind them. Governments and NGOs that once saw capitalism and consumerism as enemies of progress are discovering the virtues of free markets and entrepreneurship, with an emphasis on engaging low-income populations as customers and partners rather than passive recipients of aid and services.

C. K. Prahalad presented the most compelling case for this strategy in his 2004 bestseller, *The Fortune at the Bottom of the Pyramid: Eradicating Poverty Through Profits*,[6] which had an immediate and enormous influence on development-focused institutions such as the Gates Foundation and the Clinton Global Initiative. Mohammed Yunis,[7] the visionary advocate for micro-credit and indigenous entrepreneurship, won the Nobel Prize in 2006, drawing even more attention to the efficacy of indigenous development at the grassroots level. These "bottom of the pyramid" strategies speak boldly in the language of opportunity and empowerment to a generation bristling with enthusiasm and armed with unprecedented access to global information, resources, and markets.

EXPLORING THE RISE OF THE YOUNG WORLD

The rise of the Young World is an exciting, important story, but a complicated one to tell. Chapter 1 of this book examines the larger trends of older and younger populations, the spread of networks and technology across the globe, and the role of indigenous entrepreneurship in economic development. I try to avoid a dry recitation of facts and figures and instead use these data points to illuminate how the trends relate to and reinforce one another. Further data and discussion of these trends are provided in the Appendices.

Chapter 2 looks at how deliberate institutional investments in technology skills, subsidized equipment, and business skills, made by organizations with vested interests in the spread of knowledge economy entrepreneurship, are providing additional momentum to the trends already propelled by demographics and globalization.

Chapter 3 provides a panoramic (or, perhaps, kaleidoscopic) tour of the new global ecosystem that is spawning, incubating, and launching a growing army of Young World entrepreneurs whose methods and ambitions are steeped in digital culture and Net Generation norms. We will hear from the entrepreneurs themselves, in stories ranging from ICT training programs in the slums of Lagos to the corporate campuses of some of the world's largest and most competitive information services companies.

This section takes a closer look at the unique aspects of Young World entrepreneurship: the blend of social and commercial models, the ability to make both intensive and extensive use of social networks and mobile technology to reach the global market and the global talent pool, the evolution of new public-private-NGO partnerships based on mutual interest, and the ways that Young World entrepreneurs are filling gaps in the entrepreneurial ecosystem itself rather than waiting for top-down institutional responses to long-standing challenges.

A NOTE ON THE CASE STUDIES

The case studies in Chapter 2 (institutions) and Chapter 3 (entrepreneurs) are intended as examples of new approaches, not as "best practices" in the traditional sense. There are literally millions of people and organizations operating in this space, and I doubt that anyone can say with assurance which are the "best" or most likely to succeed. I selected these cases on the basis of extensive research and conversations because they effectively illustrate the larger concepts that were common across many of the organizations I studied. Subsequent to my research but prior to the publication of this book, some of these companies and individuals received attention from the international community, including invitations to the World Economic Forum at Davos and the TED Conference, and coverage in the media—so it's comforting to know that I was not the only one impressed by their ideas. However, the inclusion of particular companies, governments, and individuals should not be read to suggest I think these entities are necessarily unique or superior to others doing the same or similar work.

The stories in this section are drawn from some of the most intriguing initiatives on five continents, including:

- Capacity-building efforts that blend public, private, and NGO resources to increase the ICT skills base and improve the employment prospects for young talent
- Social networks for employability training, knowledge-sharing, and engaging diaspora populations
- Innovative products and services geared to solve local problems, scaled to be sustainable in resource-constrained environments
- Indigenous businesses that reach out to global markets using state-of-the-art business strategies and technologies
- Young World entrepreneurs competing at the very pinnacle of the global knowledge economy

One of the most engaging parts for me in tracing the story of the rise of the Young World is the passion, intelligence, and strategic vision of the protagonists. The case studies are drawn from extensive personal

conversations and first-hand research, with a strong emphasis on passing along the insights of the experts, practitioners and entrepreneurs
in their own voices.

Chapter 4 looks at what the rise of the Young World means for businesses, governments, and individuals as massive changes ripple through
the global value chain. Globalization and technology may be creating
opportunities, but they are also creating new competition—for jobs,
for business, for existing modes of governance, and for institutions
accustomed to positions at the top of the global hierarchy. However,
the rise of a multipolar world of business does not spell doom for multinationals or for the well-paid Old World creative class. This chapter
presents opportunities for creating win-win engagements that help
current businesses manage workforce transition and reach new markets, while providing Young World insurgents with room to grow and
innovate. Chapter 4 explores how to:

- Engage Young World Talent
- Collaborate with Young World Partners
- Invest in Young World Opportunity
- Build Young World Markets
- Plan for Uncertainty

PROMISE AND PERIL

The rise of the Young World is not a foregone conclusion. In fact,
despite all the momentum and energy documented in the forthcoming
pages, it remains an unlikely hope. The young entrepreneurs trying to
ride market forces toward a sustainable future face not only the traditional obstacles of their rugged surroundings, but also the anxieties that
their success will breed among those already established, be they local
competitors, multinationals, governments, or cultural traditionalists.

In a sense, accommodating the disruptive new approaches of the
Young World entrepreneurs into the current system of globalization is
analogous to trying to find a place for the Net Generation in workplaces dominated by competitive Baby Boomer values and anxious
Boomers paralyzed by fears of their own potential obsolescence. Transition
is inevitable, but it can be managed well or poorly. Technology can facilitate a smooth transfer of knowledge or expose underlying conflicts.

Especially at this moment—in the midst of a global recession—it's easy to view any change with alarm and interpret the "rise of the rest"[8] as necessitating somebody's decline and fall. Globalization can appear to be fulfilling its negative destiny of driving a race to the bottom, where the emergence of a vibrant IT development community in Africa, for example, means wages in the United States and Europe will sink to sub-Saharan levels. That seems to me an extreme and unlikely outcome, and if things start heading that way in earnest, we will all have bigger things to worry about.

Young World Rising considers the flip-side of globalization: as a race to the top, not a race to the bottom. Entrepreneurship is about the creation of wealth, the growth of organizations, and the ideals of meritocracy. The new kind of knowledge economy entrepreneurship made possible by information and communication technology holds even more potential than that. It is the creation of something— content, data, insight, entertainment—from nothing except human talent and imagination. From that seed can spring entire ecosystems of prosperity in concentric circles—services, goods, luxuries, public amenities, social cohesion, political stability.

Young World Rising could be seen as a threat or a promise. In this book, I choose to look at the promise.

CHAPTER 1

THE RISING TIDE

Three Trends Driving the Emergence of the Young World

The decade of the 2010s will witness the convergence of three critical trends that each exert a powerful pull on the economic trajectory of the world: the aging of the developed economies, the spread of ubiquitous data networks across the globe, and the rise of indigenous entrepreneurism as an alternative a path to economic development from the top-down economic assistance model that prevailed in the postcolonial period. These trends on their own are relatively well-known and planned-for; their interaction gives rise to profound uncertainties.

Demographers, sociologists, technologists, economists, and political scientists tend to study each of these trends in isolation. Consequently, forecasts about the future of the workforce, the future of technology, and the future of the developing world tend to reflect the siloed expertise of the individuals and institutions conducting the analysis.

In the real world, these trends are unfolding in tandem. They abut and reinforce one another at various points. These areas of overlap and interrelationship suggest strategies for businesses, governments, non-governmental organizations (NGOs) and individuals seeking to address the significant challenges of the next two decades, and they provide one set of answers to questions about the size, shape, and nature of the next generation of innovation.

DEMOGRAPHY AND DESTINY

When I was working on *Generation Blend* in 2007, I was intensely concerned with the problems caused in the workforce by the retirement of the large Baby Boom generation (around 78 million in the United States) and the lack of skilled replacements in the cohort immediately succeeding them (known as Generation X in the United States, numbering only 53 million). If the United States did not find a way to compensate for the impending loss of knowledge brought about by the retirement of the Boomers, organizations would find themselves without the skills and capabilities to perform at previous levels.

The aging workforce is a problem in the global dimension. Declining fertility rates (number of children per woman of childbearing age) correlate to rising levels of per capita income. Life spans also increase with prosperity. This dynamic means countries get older as they get richer, with fewer working-age people to support greater numbers of increasingly elderly retirees.

There is an optimum point on the growth-demographics curve where a society on the brink of economic maturity has a surfeit of working-age people available to fill new opportunities created by investment and innovation. Harvard demographer David Bloom, who studies the effects of young populations on economic development, refers to this as the "demographic dividend."[1] The effects of the demographic dividend could be seen in the rise of Japan in the 1970s, the Asian "Tiger" economies (Singapore, Taiwan, South Korea) in the 1980s, and in China's frenetic growth rate today.

By the mid-2020s, most of the developed world and China will be past the "dividend" phase and into the aging portion of the curve, many at an alarmingly steep rate. Meanwhile, today's poorer parts of the world will just be entering into the years of maximum demographic opportunity.

THE RICH OLD WORLD

The United States, Europe, and Japan experienced baby booms in the years following World War II, and the surge of young workers coming into their economies, combined with the war-thinned ranks of middle-aged and elderly, produced a demographic dividend that drove an economic expansion of unprecedented magnitude.

The resulting prosperity, along with increased participation of women in the workforce, led to a drop-off in birthrates in the next generation. In the United States, fertility rates eventually began creeping back toward replacement level (2.1 children per woman, reached in 2008); in Europe and Japan, they continued to decline, while increasing life expectancies combined with low birthrates to create a rapidly-aging population, especially at the most elderly end of the scale. See Appendix A for detailed data on the impact of aging populations worldwide.

Demographic projections even cast a pall over the otherwise-triumphant story of China's emergence as a global economic power. Today, China looks to be surging ahead of the world in output and savings. In fact, China is in a desperate race against time to get rich before it gets old. "China will be also experiencing a rapid population aging after 2015," write two labor economists at the People's University of China in a 2009 study. "One fifth to one quarter of the Chinese population would be older people at age 65 or over after 2035. The year of 2029 would be a turning point in China's age structure transition, when for the first time in Chinese history the elderly population would exceed the child population."[2]

One much-talked-about consequence of the gray tide sweeping over the developed nations are the obligations due to retirees in terms of healthcare and pension transfer payments, which aging electorates will insist that their governments honor. These threaten to place a crushing burden on the shrinking numbers of young people in the workforce, and could drag down living standards as countries disinvest trillions in accumulated capital to support mushrooming populations of elderly retirees.

There are more subtle implications as well. Old countries behave differently and have different priorities for the way they allocate resources than younger ones. Risk tolerance, ability to change direction and strategy, and innovation will all likely be affected. The transfer of skills and knowledge will consume disproportionate resources. So will the upkeep of legacy systems, obsolete practices, and outdated institutions.

Then there's the technology adoption issue. High-growth business opportunities in the knowledge economy increasingly depend on digital information systems, communication platforms, and social networks. Members of the Net Generation grew up alongside this technology and have an innate, experiential awareness of its capabilities that their pre-digital elders lack. As the technology continues to evolve and develop, with consumer technologies blending into business applications and vice versa, young people will continue to be the leading adopters and implementers. Soon, access to these systems will be nearly ubiquitous, around the globe and up and down the socioeconomic ladder. Societies with high ratios and/or high absolute numbers of young people can not only expect the traditional benefits of a demographic dividend, but also significant first-mover advantages in the application of information and communications technology (ICT) and social networks to business, politics, cultural development, and general innovation.

The bottom line is that the countries that have been the drivers of innovation and productivity for the past several centuries are running out of juice. An increasing percentage of the populations of Japan and Europe have their most productive years behind them—and their years of greatest healthcare costs ahead of them, or upon them. Even absent any other externalities, that situation creates enormous competitive challenges for any economy.

Is there hope for the rapidly aging old world? Perhaps, but it lies in discovering new markets, new sources of inspiration, and new partners in the co-creation of value. It depends, in short, on the Young World rising.

THE POOR YOUNG WORLD

Of the world's current population of 6.7 billion, more than 3 billion are under the age of 24, and many of the world's youngest populations reside in some of the world's poorest countries. Exhibit 1.1 plots selected countries on a matrix of median population age and per-capita GDP.

What's apparent from this chart is that there is an almost complete disjunction between the rich old world and the poor young world. Only oil-rich Gulf States such as Saudi Arabia and Qatar are both young and relatively prosperous. China and Russia, as noted above, are conspicuous outliers in the bottom right quadrant, as the oldest poor

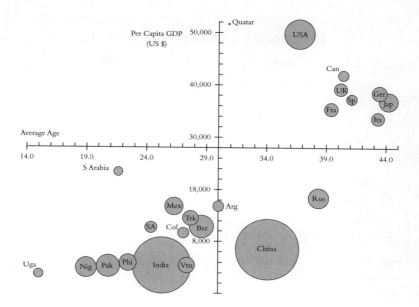

Exhibit 1.1 Age and Wealth, 2008 (size of dots roughly to scale with countries' populations)

Sources: Economist—Pocket World of Figures, 2009 Edition, Economist Intelligence Unit (www.eiu.com), World Bank—HNP Stats (www.worldbank.org). Data from 2007–2008.

country and the poorest old country respectively. The United States, by these metrics, is well-positioned both economically and demographically, especially relative to other Organization for Economic Co-operation and Development (OECD) countries.

In this book, the term *Young World* refers to the cluster of countries in the bottom left quadrant, including India, Nigeria, Mexico, Brazil, Indonesia, Colombia, South Africa, the Philippines, and Vietnam, where youthful, tech-empowered entrepreneurs have the greatest potential to drive economic growth and uplift the standards of living.

Needless to say, these are remarkably different countries and cultures in most respects. They are also exceptionally dynamic and volatile. Each has its own unique set of local uncertainties and driving forces for change, and any forecast regarding these countries as a generalized bloc will almost certainly fail to account for at least a couple of important discontinuities—natural disaster, resource depletion, political turmoil, cultural or religious developments, and so on—that will either accelerate change or knock any given country off the path of prosperity.

VANGUARDS OF THE YOUNG WORLD

Latin America
- Mexico
- Colombia
- Brazil
- Chile

Africa
- South Africa
- Ghana
- Kenya
- Nigeria

South Asia:
- India
- Vietnam
- Malaysia
- Indonesia
- Philippines

In the aggregate, however, what these countries have in common—youth, rapid adoption of new technologies, and a growing number of indigenous businesses—have a greater potential to shape their destiny than the factors that separate them. Over the next 10–25 years, the global wave of youth fueled by Young World countries will assume greater significance, either as a disruptive force pushing the world toward increased turbulence and chaos or as a new wave of cooperation uniting talent and innovation to tackle global challenges.

Rebalancing the Global Population. Though estimates are constantly being revised, a 2008 study by the United Nations[3] forecasts that the global population to peak in 2050 at somewhere between 7.79 and 10.76 billion (median: 9.2 billion) before gradually tapering off.*

---

* Note that the difference between the low and the high estimate is nearly 3 billion people, so the median estimate should be read as "9.2 billion, plus or minus the current population of China." The consequences of hitting the high number are considerably greater in all dimensions, especially in terms of resource and environmental impact. This is just one of many uncertainties that readers should keep in mind when evaluating these forecasts.

By that time, Asia (57%) and Africa (22%) will combine to represent nearly 80% of the total global population, with North America and Europe constituting a paltry 5% and 7% respectively (see Exhibit 1.2).

The disparity between the aging north and the youthful south is also expected to widen. Today, 366 million Europeans are in their working prime, age 25–59, compared with 192 million age 60 and older (Exhibit 1.3). By 2050, 281 million working-age Europeans will need to support more than 300 million retirees, including more than 66 million over the age of 80 (Exhibit 1.4).

By contrast, the working age population of Asia is projected to increase from 1.9 billion today to more than 2.4 billion in 2050, with another 645 million age 15–24 coming up behind them. Over 1.2 billion will reside in India alone, which will surpass China with the world's largest working-age population by 2030 (Exhibit 1.5). In the same timeframe, only 28% of Asians will be over age 60.

The trend of the numbers is clear. What remains uncertain is whether the Young World can take its dividend to the bank, by converting the

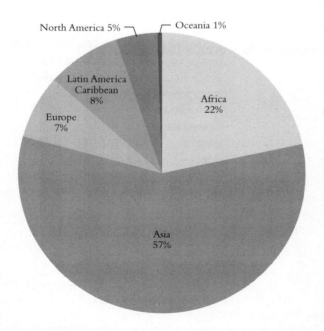

Exhibit 1.2   Regional Population Distribution in 2050 (UN forecast, 2007)

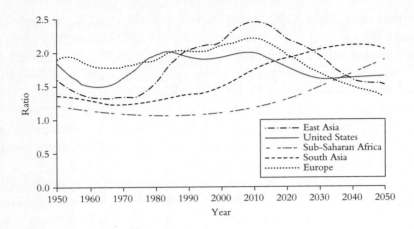

Exhibit 1.3 Ratio of Working Age to Dependent Population

sheer numbers of young people into a qualitative advantage in talent that will propel their economies forward. That will take enormous investments in education and workforce development—although, as we will see in Chapters 2 and 3, not all the investment need come from the traditional sources.

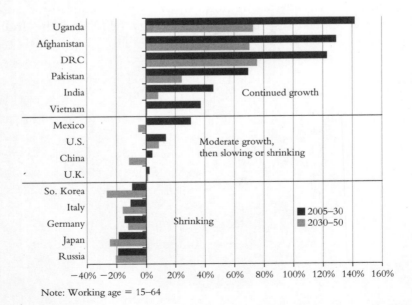

Note: Working age = 15–64

Exhibit 1.4 Change in Working Age Population, 2005–2050

Source: United Nations. *World Population Prospects, 2006 Revision,* Medium Variant.

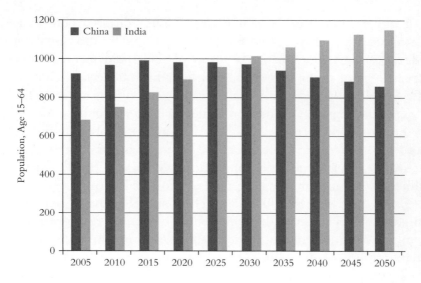

Exhibit 1.5   Working Age Population Forecast, India and China, 2005–2050
Source: U.S. Census Bureau International Database, 2009.

India Shining. In some parts of the emerging world, those investments are already taking hold. India's top tier educational institutions, the Indian Institutes of Technology (IIT) and the Indian Institutes of Management (IIM), screen their applicants with one of the world's most rigorous admissions tests, producing graduates who rank with the best of Harvard, Stanford, and MIT. Below this top tier, India's higher education system of more than 18,000 universities enrolls 11 million students per year—most of whom lack immediate qualification for employment by multinational or top-level indigenous companies, but are good candidates for training and development and provide a baseline skilled labor force for small and medium-sized businesses.

Asian Tigers Roaring. Elsewhere in Southeast Asia, Thailand is home to more than 300,000 college-educated professionals, mostly in the younger demographic, while the Philippines boasts well over half a million. The Philippines has long had one of the world's most literate populations and, with an English-speaking heritage and large numbers of overseas workers with strong ties to the homeland, shows great promise as a burgeoning center of entrepreneurism and economic development.

Latin America Faces Uneven Prospects. The educated elite in Latin America are as well-prepared as any young people for the global knowledge economy, but the distribution of skills (and income) remains especially poor in this part of the world. Latin students lag behind most of their global peers in math and reading, according to the OECD. Most of the region's 200 million Millennials are currently underskilled for employment in high-level information work jobs. Despite these barriers, Mexico and Colombia have emerged as important centers of tech-driven entrepreneurial innovation, along with Brazil and Chile, which are already far along the road to economic prosperity.

Bright Spots in Africa. While much of sub-Saharan Africa remains mired in abject poverty, the continent is beginning to produce larger numbers of educated young professionals, and investments are intensifying as part of the Millennium Development Goals articulated by the United Nations. South Africa, despite lingering inequalities, has emerged as a regional hub of economic growth and innovation, but East Africa and parts of coastal West Africa are also demonstrating more promise than they have since the earliest years of independence (see Exhibit 1.6). Nigeria, home to the world's third largest entertainment industry, is also becoming a hotbed of high-tech development, as is neighboring Ghana. Kenya, Rwanda, and Uganda are among the leaders in East Africa. These results, as we shall see, are generated almost exclusively by the efforts of young indigenous entrepreneurs.

Still Too Much Room at the Bottom. Not all the signs are hopeful. Worrisome numbers of global Millennials are coming of age in societies that lack the most rudimentary physical infrastructure: clean water, sanitation, food, shelter, access to healthcare. Sometimes these conditions are aggravated by political instability, fanaticism, and war. Afghanistan, for example, posted the fifth highest population growth rate in 2008.[4] It seems unlikely that this fact will do the country much good in the near term.

Even in areas of persistent poverty, population growth alone is not the culprit. World Bank economist Charles Kenny, who studied the issues closely, writes in the introduction to his new book, *The Success of Development*, "There is little evidence from anywhere that growing populations condemn a country to a declining standard of living. Looking at Africa in particular, while populations continue to expand, there is no link from population growth to declining income, and

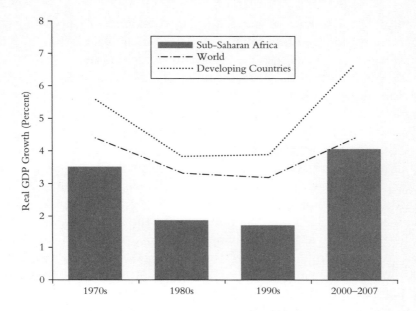

Exhibit 1.6   Economic Growth Rates in Sub-Saharan Africa Relative to World

Source: IMF *World Economic Outlook* and IMF African Department Database.

mortality rates are falling, not rising. Even if the institutions which are central to per capita growth develop slowly, the technologies required for greater output—GDP increases—spread fast. And this is enough to prevent widespread and recurring famine."[5]

Realistically, whatever promises technology and entrepreneurship might hold for young inhabitants of the very poorest and most violent corners of the globe lay further in the future than is practical to forecast from our current vantage point. Nevertheless, some of the countries that today show signs of promise were considered part of this bottom group not long ago, and have managed, through internal reforms, commercial development, and the concerted efforts of regional partners and international donors, to begin to climb toward a brighter future.

THE SPREAD OF UBIQUITOUS DATA NETWORKS

The ability of Young World countries to cash in on their demographic dividends depends in large measure on the increasing access and falling cost of information and communication technology. Networks

are not just conduits of data: they are conduits of opportunity—
opportunity for learning, for participation, for collaboration, and for
transformation. They are the means by which some of the Young
World's billions will climb to greatness and pull many of their compatriots along behind them. Fortunately, the spread of networks is
taking place concurrent with the demographic transition from Old
World to Young, driven by the logic of market forces.

The Digital Divide is Closing . . . Slowly. Connectivity to the Internet
is the ante at the table if you want to play in the knowledge economy. In 2000, there was a vast digital divide separating the developed
world, with high-income countries enjoying vastly more widespread
and higher-speed access to the Internet than the rest of the world. The
past 10 years have seen a narrowing of that gap. As of 2007, broadband
was commercially available in 166 countries, including more than
300 million subscribers in what the World Bank defines as "middle
income" countries. In 2006, 3.4% of the population in low-income
countries and 3.9% in middle-income countries has broadband, compared with 18.6% in developed economies.[6] See Appendix B for data
on the spread of connectivity around the world.

The authors of a 2009 study by the World Bank believe that
broadband has a measurable economic impact in "improving human
capital, a necessary condition for economic growth and competitiveness."[7] Consumers are better able to access the more interesting
knowledge-sharing and collaboration services that the industry calls
"Web 2.0," including blogs, wikis, social networks, voice-over-IP
(VoIP) computer telephony, video, and other activities that require
constant, fast connections to the Internet.

When Internet usage within a country reaches critical mass, it
can dramatically impact top-line measures of economic growth. In a
2006 study of 27 developed and 66 developing countries, economists
George Clarke and Scott Wallsten found that a one-percentage-point
increase in the number of Internet users is correlated with a boost
in exports of 4.3 percentage points and an increase in exports from
low-income to high-income countries of 3.8 percentage points.[8] The
World Bank calculates that "a high-income economy with an average
of 10 broadband subscribers per 100 people would have enjoyed a
1.21 percentage point increase in per capita GDP growth. This potential growth increase is substantial given that the average growth rate of
developed economies was just 2.1 percent between 1980 and 2006."[9]

Part of the limiting factor in the spread of the Internet prior to 2000 was the poor state of landline infrastructure in less-developed countries. Now wireless and satellite-based data services are reducing or eliminating dependency on landlines and bringing high-quality, low-cost connectivity to poorly served regions, including rural communities and second-tier cities that have lagged behind until now.

The Young World is Going Mobile. Another factor fueling the spread of the knowledge economy is the increased access to Internet-capable devices. Most people in mature economies connect to the Internet primarily via personal computer or full-function laptop, typically costing $500 or more—a price point that leaves a considerable percentage of the developing world on the outside looking in. Over the past several years, a number of developments have been driving that barrier down. The $100 laptop project, One Laptop Per Child, and similar efforts sponsored by nonprofit or corporate efforts have expanded PC-based connectivity options. Recent new hardware innovations like super-lightweight netbooks and smartphones with near-PC levels of functionality are bringing even higher levels of computing power within the reach of low-income communities and individuals.

Mobile telephony is the leading edge of this revolution. In 2002, the total number of mobile phones in the world surpassed the number of fixed telephones; by 2008, Wireless Intelligence reports there were an estimated four billion mobile phones globally.[10] The deployment of cellular and satellite-based networks has made at least occasional service available to people at the very lowest levels of the socioeconomic scale, and made mobile phones a requirement for anyone with ambition and aspirations, even in countries with per-capita incomes of $600 per annum or less. Since 2000, Young World countries have accounted for increasing percentages of the total number of new mobile subscribers (see Exhibit 1.7). According to forecasts by the World Bank, by 2012, almost all new subscriptions will be in emerging economies.

While the majority of cell phone users in the Young World do not yet have mobile Web access, SMS texting is nearly universal, and local providers often lead their counterparts in the developed world in creating innovative applications on the mobile platform.

Current trends indicate that the convergence between mobile usage and Web connectivity will happen extremely quickly in emerging markets. In late 2008 and early 2009, high-speed third-generation (3G) networks were introduced by the three largest service providers

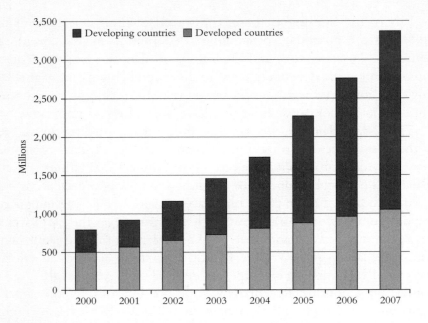

Exhibit 1.7   Mobile Phone Subscriptions in Developing and Developed Countries, 2000–2007

Source: International Telecommunication Union (ITU), World Telecommunications/ICT Indicators Database.

in India. While the cost of the plans, regulatory snarls, and the limited availability of 3G-capable handsets has so far hampered early adoption, providers look forward to mushrooming subscriptions in 2010–2011. Even in Africa, where most of the explosive growth in mobile telephony has been at the low end, Gartner reports that mobile phones with data service capabilities outnumbered the simple SMS-capable phones that dominated the continent in 2009.[11]

According to a 2008 report by Cisco Systems, mobile broadband is poised to be the next big leap forward in terms of driving Internet traffic and access (Exhibit 1.8):

Mobile operators in many parts of the world are offering mobile broadband services at prices and speeds comparable to fixed broadband. Though there are often data caps on mobile broadband services that are far lower than those of fixed, some consumers are opting to forgo their fixed lines in favor of mobile. This has a familiar ring to it from the mobile voice substitution effect that began in the late nineties and is continuing today. As a result of the mobile broadband

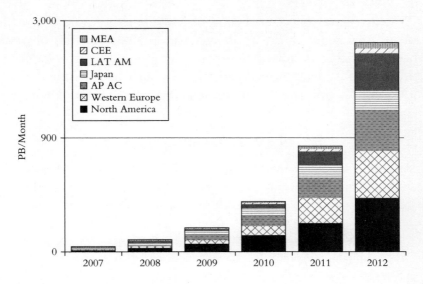

Exhibit 1.8   Mobile Broadband Forecast, 2007–2012
Source: "Approaching the Zettabyte Era." Cisco Systems Whitepaper, June, 2008.

substitution effect, Cisco is projecting very strong growth for mobile data at 120 percent CAGR from 2007 to 2012, which means that *traffic will roughly double every year.*[12]

The spread of ICT across the globe has many important social and economic implications. Its most profound effect, however, is that it is helping to galvanize more than four billion young people across the planet—including billions in the poor Young World—into a Global Net Generation, united by common attitudes and aspirations, connected and resourced on a scale never before seen in human history.

YOUTH + TECH: THE EMERGENCE OF THE GLOBAL NET GENERATION

Over the past 20 years, in mature economies, the spread of networks has influenced the social and political development of the generation born since 1980, giving rise to a number of behaviors documented by observers including Don Tapscott (*Growing Up Digital* and *Grown Up Digital*), William Strauss and Neil Howe (*Millennials Rising*), Marc Prensky ("Digital Natives and Digital Immigrants"), and myself (*Generation Blend*).

We each have our own catalog of Millennial generation traits or "norms" that seem to fit, or at least partially explain, the observed behavior of large numbers of this generation as they've established themselves as students, consumers, citizens, and now members of the workforce. The following table summarizes the common descriptors.

MILLENNIAL NORMS AND BEHAVIORS

Since the early 1990s, the Millennial generation has been the subject of study and speculation. Here are some of the common traits attributed to them by experts, sociologists, market researchers, and HR professionals:

- *Collaborative and Social*—Millennials are sharers of information and team-oriented, preferring to work and socialize in groups.
- *High Expectations*—Millennials demand transparency, integrity, and responsibility from institutions, government, employers, and one another.
- *Feedback-Driven*—Since childhood, Millennials have received constant attention and recognition for their talents and achievements. In young adulthood, they continue to look to authority figures for mentoring and guidance.
- *Inquisitive*—Millennials scrutinize the claims of employers, government, and purveyors of goods and services, eager to find connections between their life activities and a higher social purpose.
- *Customizers and Experimenters*—Millennials differentiate themselves by customizing everything from their cell phones to their bodies, and playfully mash-up cultural references to create new contexts for their experiences.
- *Blurred Boundaries*—Millennials commingle their personal and professional lives to a significant extent, and do not recognize the same sources of division and authority as their elders.
- *Sense of Urgency*—Millennials are a generation in a hurry, with respect to their own careers, their desire to make an immediate impact in society, and their perception of problems such as poverty, environmentalism, energy conservation, and political freedom, on both a global and local scale.

Naturally such broad generalizations do not apply equally to all members of the cohort. However, polls, surveys, and focus groups conducted by organizations such as the Pew Project on the Internet and Society have gone a long way toward validating the observations of experts with meaningful data. And, as we will see in the case studies in Chapter 3, these norms manifest in the unique approaches of Young World entrepreneurs, and are woven deeply into the fabric of the organizations they create.

One of the unique aspects of the Millennial generation is that it is, by and large, a global generation. Surveys indicate a remarkable commonality in attitudes among young people North and South, East and West, from the most prosperous countries to those at the fringes of the world economy. Some of this results from the global reach of popular culture and consumer culture. When Nike says "Just Do It!" the message is heard everywhere from Cape Cod to Cape Town and appeals to the same action-oriented, ambitious qualities in young people worldwide.

A growing body of data suggests that technology plays a central role in shaping the attitudes of the Net Generation, whether they reside in developed countries that were at the forefront of the information revolution or in countries where widespread Internet access is a relatively recent phenomenon. Information networks fundamentally change relationships between people, processes, and data by lowering (or obliterating) old barriers, eliminating social formalities in personal relationships, flattening hierarchical organizations, eliminating the significance of time and distance, enabling instantaneous distribution of content, ending isolation, and providing a global platform for self-expression. Exposure to them early in life profoundly influences perceptions and expectations, even among young people who do not have any special interest in or aptitude for technology.

In 2007, the Toronto-based consulting firm New Paradigm (now nGenera) conducted an online survey of nearly 6,000 young people (ages 16–30) worldwide, including more than 400 each from Mexico, Brazil, Russia, China, and India.[13] As an online survey, it by definition polled the more connected and digitally literate segments of the population, with likely correlation to higher-than-average socioeconomic and education levels.

The survey discovered that the online habits and attitudes of NetGen youth from the four emerging economies included in the poll did not differ significantly from their peers in North America, Europe, and Japan. Across the board, more than 65% of respondents from all countries said they would prefer to live without a television than without the Internet, for example. Young people from Mexico, Brazil, Russia, and India were more far likely to consider themselves early adopters of technology than those in Western Europe, North America, or China, and spent more hours per week on the Internet (or were willing to admit that they did; see Exhibit 1.9).

These digital natives are also mobile natives. More than 80% of survey respondents in Mexico, Russia, China, and India reported sending text-messages from their mobile phones in the prior month. In India, for example, mobile phones are also the platform of choice for gaming, listening to music, banking, and online commerce. In this respect, they and the other Millennials from emerging markets are ahead of their peers in Europe and especially North America, although that may be changing with the introduction of more versatile, appealing handsets like the iPhone and the increasing popularity of mobile data plans.

The New Paradigm quantitative study also delved into consumer and workplace attitudes, revealing a high degree of commonality of opinions on a range of social, economic, and lifestyle issues across

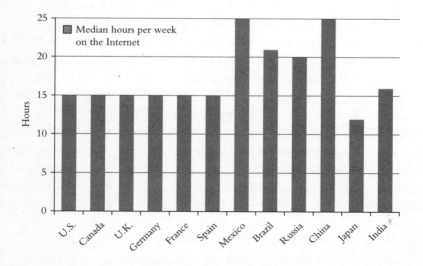

Exhibit 1.9   Age 18–30, Hours per Week Spent on the Internet

an extremely diverse geographic and economic sample. Although the methodology and nature of the survey make it difficult to draw definitive conclusions, the data point the way toward the idea that the digitally literate youth around the world have more in common with one another than they have with older and/or less connected members of their own societies.

THE TECHNOLOGY AGE GAP IN GLOBAL PERSPECTIVE

The spread of networks, digital culture, and mass collaboration affect young and old alike. However, there is a fundamental difference between those who established the habits of learning, participation, personal relationships, and work in the pre-digital world, then adapted the new technologies to fit their existing worldview, and those whose expectations and experiences are rooted exclusively in the networked digital world. While the former group tends to look at technology as a problem to be solved or a new tool to integrate into an existing framework, the latter starts with an inherent grasp of the possibilities of networks and data.

For Millennials, PCs, the Internet, mobile phones, digital music, videogames, and social networks are not novelties or innovations: They are part of the furniture. They represent the default modes of communicating, collaborating, and accessing information, against which others are judged. The linear, formal, analog processes of older generations typically strike younger people as less convenient and engaging than ones they can access instantly through networks and social channels.

Millennials have more experience using the technology than they have in the workplace or as participants in civic society, so a number of questions occur to them rooted in their personal understanding of what's possible, versus what they observe as business as usual in the workplace and the world around them.

- Why construct artificial barriers between your personal life, your professional work and your social goals, when in fact all these things are connected and reinforce each other?

- Why go through layers of management and organizational structure when it's possible to connect immediately and directly with an expert or decision-maker?
- Why work in an office when you can work just as productively from home or a coffee shop?
- Why commit to the larger goals of an employer or a government, when evidence is everywhere that institutions never live up to their stated principles?
- Why do I have to settle for my lot in life when so many other possibilities are open to me?

Pre-digital generations never considered these questions, because there were no alternatives. This was true in the industrial-age developed world, and even more so in the traditional cultures that predominate in many emerging economies. Now young people confront these choices and questions on a daily basis—and wherever in the world they live, they are coming to many of the same conclusions.

Old World Challenge: Generation Blend. In mature economies, the aspirations of the Net Generation represent a challenge for established institutions, be they cultural, political, or commercial. This vibrant, engaged, impatient, and energetic generation is emerging in the context of societies dominated by increasing numbers of older people living longer and pressing their claims for continued resources and relevance. Organizations need to balance the desire to accommodate the new and unfamiliar behavior of Net Generation workers and consumers with established ways of doing business, legacy investments, and traditional attitudes.

It's a delicate negotiation. Pre-digital generations tend to view digital technology and digital culture as disruptive—for good or for ill. Change is a problem to be solved. Digital generations accommodate pre-digital processes primarily out of courtesy to their elders; below it all, they suspect that their own methods would produce better results if not for the need to keep contact with the laggards who insist on following old rules that don't fit the current situation. Contrary to the suggestions of some observers, Millennials are indeed "backward compatible" with traditional work cultures and work practices, especially when job opportunities are scarce, but organizations that find ways to empower them in full digital-native mode tend to get greater productivity, engagement, and loyalty in return.

In politics and business, the Old World is moving across the technology age gap in fits and starts, and it will not truly reach the tipping point of Net Generation influence until well into the 2020s, when the grip of pre-digital elders on resources and authority finally loosens. The implications for the rest of the world of how aging societies handle this transition are not certain, as we will explore later.

Young World: Rising Expectations. The digital age gap also exists in the Young World, but it is far less of a problem for three important reasons. First, other gaps, such as economics, education, and literacy, are far more salient. Second, older people are more likely to reside in poorly served rural communities and less likely than younger people to be literate—an important precondition to the use of information technology. Young people, by contrast, tend to gravitate toward cities in search of better economic opportunities and consequently come into contact with relatively better communications infrastructure and more densely wired populations. Those under age 30 are more likely to have been exposed to information technology at school, in their communities, or through peers. Members of the more prosperous classes own and use technology at roughly the same rates as their counterparts elsewhere in the world and display many of the same preferences and behaviors.

And most importantly, as we've seen from the demographic data, the third reason is that there simply are not enough older people relative to younger ones to make a difference. With the exception of a very narrow stratum of elites, they don't figure into the knowledge economy in the same way that their peers do in more developed countries, where senior executive ranks of large organizations are dominated by 40- and 50-somethings.

This is not exactly breaking news. Observers of the relationship between youth and technology have been shouting "The Net Generation is a global generation!" from the rooftops for at least 10 years. However, it has an interesting corollary for countries where the steepest increases in connectivity have taken place in the past five years, rather than the last two decades: The spread of ICT turns Millennials into full-fledged members of the Net Generation. As critical mass builds in countries with high populations of young people, changes in behavior, society, and culture accelerate. Because countries that are relatively late arrivals to the online age also tend to be ones with more traditional cultures and/or isolated political systems, the incumbent predigital institutions and leadership are least equipped to deal with the kinds of change that open communication brings.

A case in point is the Twitter Revolution that swept Iran in the aftermath of the country's controversial presidential elections in June, 2009 and shook the regime to its foundations. Iran is a young, well-educated country with a high degree of Internet utilization, albeit within the social and political limits imposed by the ruling religious authorities. It also experienced a surge of new connectivity in the years leading up to the uprising. From 2005 to 2008, mobile phone subscriptions in Iran grew by more than 375%. By 2008, six of every 10 Iranians were mobile subscribers. All of these phones have SMS capabilities, and some have data access, providing their users with a conduit to the wider world that authorities could not control.[14]

Large numbers of reform-minded youth responded to President Mahmoud Ahmadinejad's suspicious claims of electoral victory with an outpouring of dissent on social media outlets such as Facebook, blogs, and Twitter. The authorities attempted all kinds of draconian measures to prevent these conversations, from blocking IP servers to shutting off mobile phone service to physically destroying computers in students' dormitories. The protesters were able to keep a step ahead of them, publishing an ongoing stream of compelling words and images primarily through Twitter, where they reached the ears of the international community and, more importantly, connected the resistance within Iran.

The openness, immediacy, and collaborative quality of social computing on the Internet was able to undo the intensive socialization of young people into the religious, cultural, and political attitudes of Iran's conservative religious leaders. The raw outrage carried in those 140-character posts to Twitter untethered the political discourse from its moorings and, through its own momentum, conjured up the possibility of a more secular democratic Iran that was unthinkable even at the extremes of acceptable political opinion within the country less than a week before. In the end, it took the full might of one of the world's most oppressive governments to suppress the uprising.*

---

* This serves to highlight another example of "Chinese exceptionalism." Just several weeks after Iran's Twitter-led uprising, the Chinese government took harsh action against the Uighur population in the western Xinjiang region. Very few firsthand accounts got out, because authorities were able to block Internet and mobile communications, which effectively hindered communication and coordination among the dissidents.

The implications of open communication and collaboration technology on totalitarian political systems are obvious beyond the need for additional elaboration, but they have nearly as much disruptive potential in the world of business and economics. The ideals of democracy, communicated via the Internet, raise the expectations that young people hold for their political leaders. The ideals of entrepreneurship—both commercial and social—raise their expectations for their own potential impact. Every day, all over the world, little revolutions are taking place that overthrow old habits of mind and old limits on the potential of people to succeed and make an impact through their own enterprise and initiative.

As young people get connected, they start to understand what's possible. They start to see role models for themselves from outside their own cultures, and templates for success that did not—indeed could not—previously occur to them. Suhas Gopinath, in Bangalore, India, took inspiration from Bill Gates (a global celebrity, to be sure), 10,000 miles away in Seattle, Washington. Even today, a 14-year-old in Brazil or Nigeria might be taking inspiration from Suhas Gopinath, whom they read about on a Web site. One of the most important efforts taking place along these lines focuses on empowering young women in traditionally patriarchal cultures, providing them with not only the skills but also the confidence to participate fully in the tech-driven business environment.

YOUTH AND ENTREPRENEURSHIP

Entrepreneurship is a natural outgrowth of youth. Young people have less to lose when pursuing their own ideas, and studies show that great innovators tend to do their most important work in their 20s and 30s. The desire to work for oneself, however, has traditionally been tempered by the realities of the business world. Young people lack life experience, and may be prone to errors of temperament and judgment. They lack the history and relationships that their elders acquire over the years, which can be decisive in building a fledgling business. They lack access to resources. Without a track record and a credit history, who would risk capital on an unproven venture with unproven leadership?

The spread of network access and the globalization of the digital economy lowers or collapses those barriers by:

- *Narrowing information gaps*: Through the Internet, young entrepreneurs have instant access to the global repository of institutional wisdom: the latest business information and strategies, including the experiences of more established companies, which can help new firms avoid the mistakes of their predecessors and capitalize immediately on best practices. They still need the discipline to apply these lessons to their own ventures, but young entrepreneurs who understand how to interpret information can leapfrog over stages of development that used to require years or decades of trial and error.

- *Automating social connections*: Online social networks make it virtually effortless for young people to connect with people and resources useful to their enterprise anywhere in the world. More and more such networks are coming online specifically for the purpose of creating opportunities for young entrepreneurs and job-seekers, as we will see in later sections. These sites automate the hard work of building up and maintaining relationships, gaining introductions to useful people, finding sponsors and mentors, spreading word-of-mouth recommendations, and getting tips that can make all the difference to success. Critics argue that the breadth afforded by social networks is no substitute for the deep trust afforded by personal connections built up over time. That may be so, but in many cases, the transient and transactional relationships facilitated by social networks deliver the same benefits faster and at lower costs to maintain, even as they create the basis for deeper, longer-term relationships over time.

- *Reducing capital requirements for certain business models*: In the global information economy, knowledge and talent can be more valuable to a small business than physical capital. Successful businesses can begin with nothing more than an idea and an Internet connection. In resource-poor Young World countries, which may lack even rudimentary infrastructure necessary to other kinds of industries and access to basic financial resources, this simple fact profoundly changes the whole conversation around economic development. It enables businesses to start and succeed at levels low enough to be sustainable even in poor conditions, with economic models appropriate to serve local populations with very limited buying power — or to gain immediate and unrestricted access to prosperous Old World consumer markets purely on the strength of better ideas and better execution.

Because of these three factors, the traditional costs and risks associated with entrepreneurship are far lower today than ever before. This, combined with the examples of conspicuous success by indigenous entrepreneurs in emerging economies, has fundamentally changed the calculus for many young people looking to improve conditions for themselves, their families, and their societies. It has also opened the floodgates of market-driven innovation as a means of improving the lives of the billions at the margins of economic development.

INNOVATION AT THE BOTTOM OF THE PYRAMID

To date, some of the most visible examples of knowledge economy entrepreneurship in emerging economies have closely resembled models in the developed world. Companies like India's Infosys have built well-resourced, highly professional organizations that mobilize their countries' best-educated talent. Their corporate campuses are oases of 21st century design and amenities amid a desert of poverty and underdevelopment. This kind of conspicuous success offers a beacon to aspiring local entrepreneurs, but until very recently, it was a path realistically open only to the elite. Now, the spread of high-speed networks and low-cost devices is opening another path.

Because so much of the Young World is so poor, a significant portion of indigenous entrepreneurial activity, both social and commercial, is focused on serving the population that business professor C. K. Prahalad refers to as the "bottom [or base] of the pyramid" (BOP): the more than 4 billion consumers making less than $2 per day.[15] This largely untapped market not only represents more aggregate buying power than the top global quintile, but is also composed of extremely shrewd consumers striving for better lives and hungry for innovative solutions to their daily problems. The genius of the "bottom of the pyramid" strategy is that it defines poverty in qualitative rather than quantitative terms and seeks to alleviate the effects of poverty by improving the value that low-income people can get for their money.

Prahalad's reframing of impoverished populations as potential consumers with an active interest in their material betterment, rather than passive recipients of aid, completely transforms the issue of inter-national economic development and creates a much larger role for commercial enterprise. Suddenly, helping the global poor find their way to better lives is not just a matter of altruism, but a win-win opportunity for businesses, consumers, communities, governments, and NGOs.

Dignity, Not Dependency. The shift in thinking has a subtle but profound impact on the mindset of young BOP populations. Rather than stigmatizing consumerism and commerce, Prahalad's formula-tion enables dignity and choice, and ennobles entrepreneurism as the ultimate expression of "doing well by doing good." Large companies exhibit respect for BOP customers by making investments in prod-ucts that fit their needs. They also demonstrate a kind of ingenuity in terms of how they approach the market, which in turn rubs off on indigenous entrepreneurs who aspire to their success.

The recognition of the kinds of commercial opportunities that exist at the bottom of the pyramid has transformed the discourse around foreign aid. In *Dead Aid: Why Aid is Not Working and How There is a Better Way for Africa*, African-born economist Dambisa Moyo challenges the prevailing mindset about the effectiveness of top-down foreign assistance for impoverished companies and sug-gests that better efforts at economic development can come from empowering local producers, local markets, and local entrepreneurs. Whether Moyo's critique is correct or not, the influence of her work indicates growing momentum behind alternative approaches to alleviating the poverty that afflicts much of the Young World, just at the moment when the rising generation is discovering new methods of expression, connection, and empowerment through ICT networks.

The challenge of serving the BOP market is that the consumers lack discretionary income. Prahalad points to numerous examples of busi-nesses that successfully overcome this problem by scaling their offerings to fit the budget and life conditions of BOP customers: single servings of products priced in the smallest local unit currency (e.g., a penny for a packet of laundry soap, rather than $3 for a box); conveniences designed for the hostile infrastructure that characterizes the living situations of most BOP populations; and brands that promise consistent quality.

Lean, Sustainable Capitalism. Making money selling products at a penny at retail means that businesses serving BOP markets have no margin for error. They must operate with extreme efficiency, and their business models must be ingeniously well-crafted. For large multinationals, scaling down takes discipline, but most can afford to absorb some losses while they get the model right.

Local entrepreneurs, however, often start at the bottom. They need to figure out ways to make money under conditions of extreme scarcity from day one. Even if they have access to capital and technology, their immediate customers may not. The products and services they deliver must therefore provide competitive value in the absence of practically all the assumptions that apply in mature markets. They have to be durable, high-quality, convenient to obtain, easy to use, and available at an almost unimaginably low unit cost. The production process necessitated by such conditions is lean in ways that are well-adapted for a resource-constrained future. BOP entrepreneurs are not only tapping a gigantic global market, they are also at the forefront of sustainability.

The result of these strategies broadens the access that poor people have to higher quality products and services, even at low levels of income, while avoiding the economic distortions and moral hazard of direct subsidies. In India, indigenous companies are making a profit providing Lasik eye surgeries at $50, building cars that cost $2,000, and selling nationwide mobile phone service at less than 1 rupee per call (about two cents U.S.). The same is true in Africa, Latin America, and across the Young World. Each time one of these companies succeeds, it spawns an ecosystem of partners and suppliers and contributes to the maturation of local markets, infrastructure, and workforce capacity.

Just consider for a moment how lean, smart, and fast a company has to be to execute under those constraints. Now imagine how formidable such a company could be with access to capital, market visibility, and consumers with enough resources to support higher profit margins. These kinds of companies are poised to compete with the top-heavy, resource-intensive firms of the Old World.

TECHNOLOGY AND INDIGENOUS ENTREPRENEURS

Young World entrepreneurs whose business models are optimized to make money under the most hostile conditions are now suddenly able to take their wares directly to prosperous customers in the developed world through the medium of the Internet. They also have the same access to the world's most advanced technology and the world's best information.

Not every Young World enterprise is well-positioned to take advantage of these factors. Manufacturing companies, for example, are dependent on capital, physical infrastructure, local labor, government regulation, and business relationships across the global supply chain. Even the leanest, smartest, most efficient manufacturer in Nigeria is hostage to the irregularities of the power grid, bad roads, corrupt officials and a host of other barriers that make it difficult to break into the global market. Such a supplier could realistically compete only on the basis of extraordinarily low labor costs or the promise of cutting corners on environmental standards, workplace safety, and so on—savings that offset the high ambient costs and risks in the business environment. While economic realities will always create opportunities for these kinds of operations, they are not good models for sustainable development.

Knowledge-based businesses have none of these limitations. Once information devices become cheap enough and connectivity becomes ubiquitous and reliable—and we have seen that trends are headed in that direction, even in some of the poorest regions of the planet—the only capital you need to provide content or services on the Internet is between your ears.

Platforms Boost Prospects. Young World knowledge entrepreneurs have immediate and direct access to developed world markets. Popular technologies such as Microsoft Windows, the Apple iPhone, and Facebook provide readymade platforms for application developers and readymade distribution channels that leverage the trust of their brands to bring independently developed products and services to consumers.

In theory, any application that can meet Apple's quality standards can get listed in the iPhone App Store.* Then it's up to consumers to decide, largely on the basis of a transparent system of user ratings, whether it's worth buying.

Huge, resource-intensive developers have the advantage of familiar brands to drive sales and highly productive workforces to develop new products, but they must find the economics of selling iPhone versions of heavyweight platform games at price points as low as $4.99 challenging. By contrast, providers accustomed to delivering lean, lightweight, useful and simple products for BOP markets at low cost enjoy huge advantages. For one thing, their cost-basis for development is almost certainly lower. For another, the marginal return on capital is significantly higher, because even small profits denominated in strong, developed-world currencies have enormous buying power in the local economy. Ninety-nine cents for an iPhone application is a trivial expense to Old World consumers, but a developer in Kenya can feed her family on the money she makes from three or four downloads per day.

Capacity and Infrastructure Are Forming. Because the path of ICT-led development holds such promise, it is the focus of a number of initiatives by governments, NGOs, and, increasingly, private businesses interested in fostering economic growth in less-developed countries. Across the Americas, Africa, and South Asia, organizations of all kinds are pouring resources into technology education, skills and capacity-building; connectivity; community-based technology centers; and e-services that build information-based skills into interactions with government, healthcare, and daily activities.

At the same time, in tandem with globalization, access to credit is spreading to small businesses and individuals at the periphery of the world economy. Mobile banking is the fastest-growing technology in Africa and parts of Asia, providing financial services to huge swaths of the population that have never had access to interest-bearing savings or credit beyond the most informal local and family-based channels. As the first wave of microfinance investments bear fruit, private equity

---

* I say "in theory," because Apple's selection criteria are rather opaque. As of this writing, several competing smartphone platforms are coming to market with more open application stores, which may broaden opportunities for developers even further.

and venture capital is starting to appear to help nascent firms scale up to serve regional, national, and even global markets.

Not all of these initiatives are top-down. Increasingly, young knowledge professionals in emerging economies are communicating and collaborating via self-organized online communities and social networks and actively participating in local efforts to build ICT capacity. These efforts represent a robust blend of altruism and self-interest. Making progress against the dire social and economic conditions that prevail in many parts of the Young World is a fundamental humanitarian priority. At the same time, no one benefits more from a skilled and empowered local workforce than local employers seeking to expand their businesses.

THE INFLECTION POINT

The three major trends of demographics, technology, and entrepreneurship are peaking simultaneously, offering an unexpected path forward from the global recession of 2008–2010. All over the world, young people are seizing the opportunities presented by this unique convergence of circumstances to participate as full partners in solving common problems. Successful local entrepreneurs are reinvesting in their communities and giving employment to others. NGOs are partnering with multinational companies and local governments to build capacity that can bring underdeveloped areas surging into the knowledge economy. Networks enable conscientious young people to transcend old limitations and reach out to one another across the boundaries of culture, pressing their demands for change and real solutions.

The next chapter looks at how these trends are being reinforced through massive investments of institutional resources, motivated by a unique alignment of incentives, opportunities, and social goals.

CHAPTER 2

LAYING THE GROUNDWORK

Aligning Institutional Investments with Young World Development Goals

Knowledge-economy entrepreneurship in the Young World is on an upward trajectory for more reasons than the convergence of vast, impersonal trends like demographics, technology innovation, globalization, and market-based ideas for international development. It is also being pushed along by the deliberate efforts of governments, multinational corporations, and non-governmental organizations (NGOs). These large institutions have very different top-line agendas but nevertheless share a common interest, and they are joining forces in interesting ways to provide the training, support, and infrastructure development that prepares the field for a bumper crop of new Young World knowledge-based businesses.

Investing in computers and technology may seem like a quixotic approach to development in countries where so many basic needs are more pressing. Many of Young World countries still lack dependable sources of food, fresh water, healthcare, sanitation, and electricity. They are plagued by weak governance, corruption, underdeveloped infrastructure, and poor access to credit. Why start with an apparent luxury like high-tech skills and equipment before addressing the basics? It's a legitimate question.

Unfortunately, the record of government-centric foreign aid actually solving any of the serious development problems over the past 50 years is mixed at best.[1] Aid still has an important role to play in crisis relief and coordination, but the long-term problems hampering Young World countries are rooted in situations that can ultimately only be addressed by people within those societies. Many within the development community are now focused on building up the local capacity to address those issues, rather than pouring money from the outside to fix things that will only break again once the money runs out.

It used to be the case that you could not separate the business-oriented problem of capacity-building from the larger and more intractable problems of governance, political stability, underdevelopment, the legacy of colonialism, and so on that beset so many Young World countries. Information and communications technology (ICT) has not solved those problems, but it plays a critical role in empowering a new breed of Young World organizations and entrepreneurs to try different solutions and rapidly scale up the ones that work.

It also creates a new path to prosperity for indigenous businesses, with benefits that ripple through the entire society. New businesses create employment opportunities and a demand for skills, and drive an updraft of expectations on both governments and large businesses. This eventually builds a middle class independent of public-sector patronage and disdainful of corruption, with stable aspirations and buying power. Foreign aid cannot do that. Neither can the public sector. Only entrepreneurs can. Entrepreneurs exist in all societies and can prosper in the most adverse conditions. What's needed are governments and foreign donors supporting policies that channel entrepreneurial energy into the creation of legitimate businesses rather than illicit or informal ones.

Investments in ICT capacity-building can provide indigenous entrepreneurs with a new way to create wealth and value: one less dependent on external conditions and capital than, say, mining, but which benefits greatly from increases in education, computer literacy, intellectual property protection, and communications infrastructure. Indigenous ICT entrepreneurs not only become drivers of prosperity because of the relatively high value of their services on the global market, but they also become strong internal advocates for transparent government, good education and stable markets. Examples in Chapter 3 demonstrate that clearly.

In the long run, the advocacy and engagement of internal constituencies within Young World countries are the only things that will allow them to transcend post-Colonial dependency on foreign aid and address the longstanding problems that perpetuate them in conditions of poverty and underdevelopment. Buying computers for poor countries and training local youth to use them may not directly "solve" hunger or corruption, but it empowers the only people who can.

Beyond Good Intentions. What makes today's institutional support for knowledge-economy and ICT-based development different from more general corporate "social responsibility" is that it is not only dependent on good will, humanitarian sentiment, public relations and general corporate citizenship. Those lofty, long-term goals happen to align with the tactical, immediate objectives at the heart of the various institutional missions: reaching new markets in the case of corporations; aggrandizing the national interest and keeping the public happy in the case of governments; and achieving visible successes for sponsors in the case of NGOs.

Consider the case of Portugal's Magellan project, discussed in more detail later in the chapter. Giving out free or heavily subsidized laptop computers to school children makes sense for the government of Portugal because it provides citizens with a tangible benefit, provides macroeconomic stimulus for the national economy, improves educational prospects for the next generation, and pleases a valuable constituency—the telecom providers—by giving them nearly a million new customers for mobile data services. It makes sense for suppliers like Intel and Microsoft, who get to put their products in front of a whole generation of impressionable young consumers, even at the loss of some profit margin. And it makes sense for education advocates and nonprofit groups like One Laptop Per Child, who benefit from a large scale proof-of-concept even if they are not directly involved in the deployment. As a byproduct, hundreds of thousands of young people get access to the wide world of information and knowledge networks, creating a critical mass of potential for new innovation and new business creation. Yes, that was the stated goal in the first place, but it is much more likely to actually happen because every institutional stakeholder in the program has a pragmatic as well as an altruistic reason to participate.

ICT-based development programs also have the benefit of being exciting, sexy, and tied in to the marketing efforts of the high-tech industry to make sure that image stays fresh. The young people who are the targets of these programs don't need to be told why laptops and the Internet are cool. There's no "eat your vegetables" or "just say no" propaganda required. As a result, the programs serve an enthusiastic constituency of participants, not a reluctant clientele of dependents and victims.

Institutional investments in ICT-based capacity building are also more targeted, more strategic, and more sophisticated in linking efforts to outcomes rather than intentions. Groups are partnering with each other in new ways and working closely with local partners, including many indigenous entrepreneurs, as we will see in Chapter 3. All of this suggests that these types of programs are more likely to meet with success in their immediate objectives—education, access, workforce development, and small business incubation—while laying the groundwork for more dramatic systemic transformation through the explosion of Young World knowledge economy entrepreneurship.

The diverse examples of Microsoft's Unlimited Potential Program, the government of Portugal's Magellan Initiative, and the Young Americas Business Trust all demonstrate how institutional resources, smartly deployed, can support bottom-up capacity-building without smothering it under layers of bureaucracy.

ALIGNING PROFIT AND PROSPERITY: MICROSOFT UNLIMITED POTENTIAL (UNITED STATES/GLOBAL)

NGOs that foster economic development are common across the world, but those that are focused on ICT capacity-building have a unique advantage in finding corporate funding partners, because their social objectives are directly aligned with the business imperatives of some of the largest and best-resourced companies on earth. The high tech industry depends on educated customers to buy its products. To companies like Microsoft, Intel, Cisco, HP, and Dell Computers, corporate investments in education, workforce development, ICT infrastructure (via discounted hardware, software, equipment, and support), and even marketing assistance to local partners are not just feel-good corporate citizenship initiatives, but necessary measures to move emerging markets forward on the maturation curve to the point where they become viable customers for branded, high-end technology offerings.

Gaining an edge in these markets is imperative to continued growth in the industry. In 2008, Gartner Research estimated that IT spending in the emerging markets will grow at a combined annual growth rate of 9.9% through 2011—more than double the estimated CAGR of 4.6% for mature markets.[2]

High-tech companies are very aware of the demographic projections, the growth potential of emerging economies, and the blue-sky opportunities that new markets present. From their perspective, it is never too early to begin the battle for market share and mindshare. A few strategic investments in ICT capacity-building can yield a bountiful crop once emerging markets mature and their knowledge economy sectors start to grow in earnest. In the Young World, however, global commercial software businesses face competition from their traditional multinational adversaries, from low-cost local companies (some of whom may be government subsidized), from free open source software, and from pirated versions of their own products. The multinationals can use their leverage and scale to influence large enterprises and the awarding of government contracts (especially those tied to foreign aid), but have less sway over the mid-market and small to medium business space, where most of the entrepreneurial activity is taking place. Many players in the global IT industry view it as absolutely essential to the long-term survival of branded, commercial software and hardware to establish differentiated value for their products, lest cost-conscious Young World customers ignore them in favor of cheaper options.

This is not to say that the corporations participating in capacity-building efforts and partnering with NGOs and governments are exclusively self-serving, or that there are not individuals within those companies deeply committed to social objectives. However, in a market economy, most businesses lack the right mechanisms to measure and reward the soft benefits of corporate citizenship. When it comes time to tighten the belt, "feel-good" programs whose only justification is PR value are more vulnerable to budget cuts than programs perceived to contribute directly to bottom-line results. In this case, ICT-centered corporate citizenship initiatives by ICT companies do double duty as strategic investments in new market growth, and are easier to defend in the boardroom on purely financial terms. The powerful alignment of market and social interests ensures that hardware, software, and equipment companies are among the most eager and reliable partners to governments, NGOs, and local businesses pursuing ICT-based development strategies.

Microsoft Corporation, the world's largest software company, has engaged the Young World through several high-profile programs: Partners in Learning, Partners for Technology Access, and The Microsoft Unlimited Potential Program. Partners in Learning (PiL) provides resources and assistance to schools, ministries of education, and local NGOs focused on teaching computer literacy to young people. Partners for Technology Access (PTA) builds public-private partnerships between various stakeholders and levels of government around education, e-government, and public engagement. Unlimited Potential (UP) invests more broadly in helping indigenous businesses, NGOs, and entrepreneurs build the capacity of the entire ICT ecosystem: technical skills, business skills, civic society, legal infrastructure (especially respect for intellectual property and anti-cybercrime programs), and demand generation.

"Microsoft has an important role to play in helping to advance social and economic opportunities in the communities where we work, live, and do business," said Microsoft CEO Steve Ballmer. "It's important that the business, government, community organizations, and individuals work together to provide the training, infrastructure, and technology that enable expanded opportunities and sustainable economic growth and prosperity."

Typically, Microsoft initiatives revolve around Microsoft technology, including some software applications that have been developed specifically around base-of-the-pyramid (BOP) needs. For example, one product, Microsoft MultiPoint, enables an entire classroom to share one PC and monitor. Microsoft has deployed this as part of its Partners in Learning program, and cites the example of an elementary school in downtown Bangkok, Thailand, where students and teachers are using the product as part of a pilot program.[3]

In another example, Microsoft has engaged with Morocco-based Assoclic, a partnership between NGOs and private companies, to provide software training via refurbished PCs in cybercafés in lower-income areas. One program in the ancient city of Fez focuses on access for the disabled.[4] The company also touts similar efforts in Brazil, this time through a partnership between community-based NGO Oxigenio and the Brazilian Ministry of Labor, aimed at developing computer skills for disadvantaged youth to increase their employability.[5] This is an initiative of some importance to Microsoft, as the government of Brazil is one of the world's leading proponents of open source software that directly competes with the company's commercially licensed offerings.

From Microsoft's perspective, these success stories do more than just burnish its public image. Having a lot of Microsoft-certified people and businesses in a particular country makes Microsoft look like the frontrunner in the local market, which influences the buying decisions of businesses who do not want to take risks on second-tier providers. It's also an advantage for consumers to use your products as a baseline for comparing with others in the market, such that different implementations favored by other software developers appear nonstandard and difficult to learn.

The company's high profile in the global IT arena has significant economic impact. According to a study by the analyst firm IDC, Microsoft's ecosystem of partners, including hardware, software, services, and related companies, was projected to invest as much as $120 billion in their local economies in 2008. This ecosystem accounted for 42% of total IT employment worldwide.[6]

By virtue of its unique position in the IT value chain, Microsoft's investments to promote its own products and technologies through education and capacity-building generate benefits that extend well beyond its corporate interests or even its industry. Some level of knowledge of Microsoft products is extremely valuable to everyone, from software developers to ordinary office workers. Doing business with a Microsoft-certified programmer, reseller, or independent software vendor (ISV) partner guarantees to prospective customers that the individual or business has met an objective standard of technical competency. In a high-risk market, that kind of seal of approval carries enormous value for the developer and the customer. Even amounts of marketing assistance that are tiny by Microsoft's standards can help local partners stand head and shoulders above their competitors.

These benefits are real and substantial, and they accrue to individuals, communities, and local businesses at least as much as to the corporate sponsors. As ICT ecosystems mature, the productivity of the entire knowledge economy improves, with ripple effects that can have a dramatic impact on the economic fortunes of entire nations. People with computer skills are qualified for better-paid jobs under better working conditions, either locally or globally. Businesses become more competitive as they deploy ICT to improve the efficiency of their internal processes, have better tools to develop new products and services, and have better channels to engage customers. They are also better able to support and extend their technology investments, because there are trained, qualified local people on hand to assist them. In the best case, this creates an updraft of prosperity that reverberates through the entire economy, driven by the increased levels of demand and elevated buying power of ICT-empowered knowledge workers and the job-creating power of the knowledge economy sector.

Once this dynamic is set in motion, there is no guarantee that any one high-tech company will benefit in a direct way. Governments and ICT-based businesses in emerging economies are looking at open source software, for example, as a pragmatic alternative to commercial products with higher per-seat license costs. As Young World consumers and businesses become more sophisticated about IT capabilities, some of them will become as critical, demanding, and fickle as their peers in established markets. Software makers like Microsoft hope that rising levels of prosperity will eventually reduce piracy and create incentives for governments to support intellectual property policies that benefit commercial developers (a topic of great importance to Microsoft, and considered part of its emerging markets strategy), but it's by no means certain. They could be making all these investments and end up developing fertile markets for their *competitors'* products.

Still, the greater risk is in allowing others to gain a foothold in important growth areas. Investments in ICT capacity-building across the Young World are something of an arms-race among the big multinational vendors: Despite the costs of engagement, no one wants to blink first, and the tendency is to escalate with bigger and better programs, rather than to retrench. The beneficiaries are local consumers, local businesses, and local entrepreneurs.

BUILDING A PUBLIC-PRIVATE PARTNERSHIP TO EQUIP THE GLOBAL NET GENERATION WITH WORLD-CLASS TECHNOLOGY: MAGELLAN INITIATIVE (PORTUGAL)

In addition to the skills gap, there is a basic issue with technology access in the Young World: Good computers and fast connections are expensive. When you don't have enough money for basic needs like food, water, and shelter, information-age appliances seem like unaffordable luxuries. In recent years, the ongoing build-out of networks and the falling price of processing power and memory have brought the price of good quality computers nearly within reach of Young World budgets. Now, a combination of philanthropy, enlightened self-interest on the part of ICT companies, and well-designed government programs is going the last mile to equip the global Net Generation with good quality hardware, software, and connectivity to fully participate in the knowledge economy.

The idea of providing free or low-cost computers to students in developing countries has been around since the mid-1990s and is one of the strategic pillars of knowledge economy capacity-building in the Young World. Educational futurists Seymour Papert, Alan Kay, and Nicolas Negroponte first outlined the concept of One Laptop Per Child (OLPC) at a conference at MIT's Media Lab in 1997. The idea matured into a full-blown initiative at the 2005 World Economic Forum in Davos, Switzerland, and is now the focus of a nonprofit foundation.

OLPC aims to bring together governments, NGOs, technology industry stakeholders, and educators to design a simple, standard laptop suitable to the needs of young people in emerging countries, at a price-point that low-income people (and low-income countries) can afford. OLPC has experienced some successes with its very low-cost, open source (Linux-based) devices in some very poor countries, where deployments were largely underwritten by foreign donors. Ironically, the most successful effort to implement the principles of OLPC has

OLPC reports the following volume of orders for the XO laptop as of August, 2009:

Country	XOs delivered, shipped and ordered
Uruguay	202,000
Peru	145,000
Mexico	50,000
UK (Birmingham)	14,000
Haiti	13,000
Afghanistan	11,000
Mongolia	10,100
Rwanda	10,000
Oceania	5,000
Paraguay	4,000

Exhibit 2.1 Top 10 One Laptop Per Child Deployments, 2009

Source: According to the One Laptop Per Child Web site, http://wiki.laptop.org/go/Deployments, accessed August 20, 2009.

occurred outside the auspices of the organization itself, as shown in Exhibit 2.1.

Portugal is not a young country, and not just in the sense of its long history. Even within the EU, it has one of the most rapidly aging populations and lowest birthrates. Nevertheless, starting in 2005, it launched the most audacious and large-scale effort at ICT capacity-building anywhere in the world, distributing more than a million laptop computers at subsidized rates to students throughout the country as part of a comprehensive effort to prepare its workforce for the knowledge economy and close a persistent digital divide.

The laptop project, named *Magellan* after the famed 15th-century explorer, was the solution to several related challenges facing incoming Prime Minister José Sócrates in 2005. First, Portugal was mired in an economic downturn and lagged its EU counterparts in technology-led economic development. Second, millions of euros in "knowledge economy investments" committed by Portuguese telecom operators as part of the 2000 auction of 3G licenses remained uncollected.

Finally, the country that had lent its capital's name to the Lisbon Agenda for European knowledge economy development faced an enormous digital divide along economic lines, with lower-income families unable to afford computers or Internet connections. Not only were most young Portuguese not getting access to 21st-century technologies in school, but the country also has a large population who came of age during the dictatorship period (ending in 1974), when educational policies left them poorly prepared for the information economy. For Portugal, workforce development is not a theoretical problem for the future; it is a very real issue in the here and now.

The Sócrates government authorized the use of the 3G auction proceeds to subsidize the distribution of nearly a million laptops before the end of the decade. This pleased the telecom providers, because it amounted to a direct investment in market development: All those students and their families would become mobile broadband customers. It provided much-needed stimulus to the local IT industry, with Portuguese OEMs contracted to manufacture the laptops and provide service and support. Most of all, it instantly leapfrogged the country's education system to the forefront of the global effort to integrate the Internet into the classroom, and promised a quantum leap forward for the country's next generation of citizens, workers, and leaders.

The scale of the project attracted IT heavyweights Microsoft and Intel, both of whom were left out of the initial OLPC designs in favor of competitors who offered discounted pricing on hardware and software. As industry leaders, the two companies felt it was important to be part of such a high-profile effort, and to gain competency and visibility for future initiatives that would inevitably happen elsewhere in the world.

The Magellan laptops come in three basic configurations: Escola, the mainstream version for 5th to 12th graders; Escolinha, a rugged tablet-format device for younger students age 6–10; and Professor, for teachers and adults in continuing education programs. Each of the three largest telecom providers offers their own models and configurations at different price-points, adhering to basic configuration standards set by the government, all available from a central Web site.[7]

With the subsidies, the end-cost to students' families is only 50–150 Euros for laptops that would sell for more than four times that amount. Qualified low-income families receive theirs for free. The Escola computers come with a one-year mobile broadband contract for 17 Euros per month (discounted from the normal 23 Euros), and other plans are negotiable depending on the providers.

Rui Grilo is Deputy Coordinator of the Technological Plan at the Cabinet-level bureau leading Portugal's knowledge economy initiatives, with enough credibility in the Portuguese high-tech community to convince even skeptical IT professionals when questions arise about the government's strategy or competence to administer such an ambitious technology initiative. I've met him on several occasions at conferences organized by Don Tapscott's organization, nGenera.

Grilo is a passionate believer in the potential of the Net Generation as a world-changing force. He acknowledged that the program was controversial in some quarters, as experts second-guessed various aspects of the technical and policy implementation, the choice of vendors, the structure of the subsidies, and the transparency of the decision-making process. Technology professionals are opinionated; politicians are opinionated. When you try to drive agreement between the two around such an ambitious plan, disputes will arise. However, Grilo believes that two main factors helped Portugal's initiative succeed where other OLPC efforts have stalled.

"It is most important to have scale," said Grilo. "It can't be just a pilot project confined to a small community. It must be everyone at once. That way, you have maximum cultural impact. Everyone feels part of the mainstream, not an anomaly or a test subject."

In terms of sheer scale, the program is an unprecedented success. Portugal deployed nearly 600,000 of the primary Escola models and 370,000 of the Escolinha laptops by June 2009. OLPC, which operates primarily in less well-resourced markets than Portugal, typically deals in implementations of 5,000 to 20,000, although both Peru and Uruguay have placed orders in excess of 290,000.[8]

One additional benefit Grilo sees in the massive scale of the program is the opportunity for mass collaboration, as teachers, students, families, and local governments experiment and trade ideas on the best solutions for integrating the new devices into the classroom and into the learning curriculum. "It must happen this way. We cannot use old command-and-control methods and hope to succeed."

The second critical factor, according to Grilo, is to "not compromise on the quality of the product." Each of the devices is built on state-of-the-art hardware providing performance comparable to mainstream laptops. Even the Escolinha "magalhaes" laptops for elementary school students feature a rugged, full-feature design based on the Intel Classmate II and a dual boot system that offers Linux and Windows XP environments. "We felt very strongly that people need a choice," said Grilo.

Perhaps the most important lesson for countries seeking to emulate Portugal's success is to design a policy that aligns the interests of all the major stakeholders: telecom providers, local OEMs, multinational partners, government ministries, local communities, schools, and the public.

When everyone has a stake in success, the project is less likely to get derailed by infighting and politics. In much of the Young World, central governments do not have the same capabilities, resources, transparency, or prestige as that of a middle-class European democracy like Portugal. Consequently, NGOs may need to play more of a role in coordination and distribution. Fortunately, they benefit from sharing common interests with some very large, well-resourced partners with a vested interest in the rapid maturation of Young World as markets for their technology products.

CONNECTING YOUNG WORLD INNOVATORS TO RESOURCES FOR INCUBATION AND BUSINESS DEVELOPMENT: YOUNG AMERICAS BUSINESS TRUST (AMERICAS)

One of the most important developments in the past decade has been the growth of NGOs and business groups dedicated to helping Young World entrepreneurs take their ideas to the next level by providing the support, attention and resources that are not available locally. These NGOs often have a transnational or regional focus, and connect with entrepreneurs via the Internet. Their efforts can springboard powerful new ideas from the most distant frontiers of innovation directly to the attention of a global ecosystem of funders, business development experts, government and NGO resources, and partnerships.

The Young Americas Business Trust (YABT) is one such group.[9] The nonprofit was founded by Roy Thomasson in cooperation with the Organization of American States (OAS) in 1999 to create opportunity for young people to access the labor market through entrepreneurship and promote business creation throughout Central and South America and the Caribbean.

Each year, YABT sponsors the Talent and Innovation Competition of the Americas (TIC Americas), where teams of young entrepreneurs present prototypes and business plans for new ventures. At stake is a modest monetary prize, plus the invaluable opportunity to attract the attention of new investors, customers, and partners.

Luis Viguria has been with the organization since 2002 and is currently the Executive Director. Born and raised in Peru, he heads a multinational team of young professionals from around the hemisphere. He spoke to me from YABT's offices in Washington, D.C.

"In Latin America and the Caribbean, our young people are very creative, they are very innovative, they have great ideas," said Viguria. "And we believe that because they are young, they don't have many chances. So we decided to create TIC Americas to give young people the opportunity not only to showcase their ideas and provide help in implementing them, but also to connect with two very important stakeholders: the government and [the financial community], including the big CEOs of the region."

Since the competition was launched in 2007, it has received thousands of applications from dozens of countries throughout the hemisphere. The online semifinals offer opportunities for young entrepreneurs to participate in training, mentorship, online resources, and free access to development software to build their business Web page (required for all entrants). The 20–30 finalists selected from the pool of more than 900 applicants get to display and advertise their products in international events such as the Private Sector Forum and the OAS General Assembly.

Almost all of the entries are either directly ICT-related or are heavily dependent on ICT for the success of their business models. Viguria said that's no accident. "The way the technology is evolving right now is very important for the development of new business. Also, young people are very likely to adapt to the new technologies; they use it as much as possible. Every time we do call for proposals, most of them are technology based."

YABT Technical Director Yerutí Méndez added that the existence of readymade global platforms for the distribution of new technology products is one of the big factors fueling ICT-based entrepreneurship in the Americas. "One of our TIC Americas participants is from Mexico. They competed last year [2008], and they are now Web developers for Apple, for iPhone applications. And that's a huge step for them because they were, I am sorry to say, nobody before the

SELECTED TIC AMERICAS INNOVATION AWARD
FINALISTS, 2007–2009

- *Aboquete* (Panama), which recycles urban and industrial organic waste to produce renewable energy and organic fertilizer
- *AgroSens* (Mexico), makers of wireless sensor networks for vineyards and high-precision agriculture
- *Bahareque* (Colombia), building affordable housing using renewable resources and environmentally sound practices
- *BNI* (Nicaragua), replacing dangerous kerosene-burning lamps with efficient, solar-powered LEDs for rural families without electricity
- *CELBIT* (Colombia), makers of a personal medical monitoring device for patients with cardiac disease
- *Dosimed* (Mexico), designers and developers of a digital drug dispenser to help patients organize and keep track of their medication regimens
- *EdgeIT* (Brazil), developers of software for media asset management optimized for delivery to mobile phones
- *Incegroup* (St. Vincent and Grenadines), a software and systems integrator
- *Ipublicity* (Bolivia), developers of a new baggage handling system for airlines called X-track
- *LasPartes.Com* (Colombia), an online marketplace for auto parts
- *MLC* (Colombia), creating educational software for special-needs children
- *Mulianuncios* (Panama), creating and commercializing solar-powered billboards
- *NutriRed* (Mexico), a social network for nutrition professionals and patients
- *Pura Applied Art* (Peru), keeping pre-Colombian designs alive in contemporary textile products
- *TLC Group* (Panama), providing updated information on trade and tariff regulations to facilitate international transactions between small and medium businesses in developing countries
- *Virita* (Mexico), a security company building auto theft solutions using GPS and cellular technology

competition. But they got so successful and they are being contacted from every single part of the world, just because they have a particular thing that made them different from other Web developers."

YABT encourages innovation, but it is at least as interested in helping regional innovators successfully commercialize their products and build their businesses. Unlike other competitions, TIC Americas requires participants to submit both a product concept and a complete business plan. All competing teams must have a project director, financial manager, and technical manager to balance vision, technical ingenuity and operational wherewithal.

"TIC Americas is not just a business plan competition," said Méndez. "We promote implementation as well. We incorporate a prototype stage for the young people before doing the business plan. They need to build a prototype, take it to the market, and if the market accepts it, then we're talking about business ideas. If not, they need to reformulate it, keep working on that and come back for a new chance. At the finals, we don't go with ideas or products: We go with real businesses looking for business opportunities, looking for market opportunities, looking for partners or investors. Once you participate in TIC Americas, you become a member of a huge network of opportunities."

Méndez said that some of the finalists from the 2007 competition received financing and support from Silicon Valley organizations in Miami, and finalists in subsequent years are way ahead of the curve in generating seed money because of the enhanced exposure.

"They want these resources. They need resources," said Viguria. "Finance is a big problem [in the Americas]. The financial sector doesn't give money to young people because they are too risky or too expensive. That's something we're trying to fight with TIC Americas: to showcase to the financial sector that investments in our young people will pay back. We need to give them the chance."

Viguria said Colombia and Mexico are traditionally the best-represented countries in the competition because of the receptiveness of those cultures to entrepreneurship and the support provided by academic and government sources. Because other countries in the region do not have the same advantages, some capacity-building is necessary. "If the entrepreneur doesn't have a resource and somewhere to go and ask questions, that's a problem," said Méndez. "So we also have several programs besides TIC Americas [to provide additional support]. One of them is called Next Links, in which we develop and train staff to help those young entrepreneurs so they will have a resource on whom to call or contact if they need a lawyer, an accountant, or if they need at least somebody to check their business funds."

Lack of coordination, according to Viguria, is a major challenge. "One problem we have in our countries is that people do not know where to find information or how to use it. There may be resources nearby geographically, but there is no coordination: A needs to work with B and B needs to work with C, but sometimes in our region, they don't cooperate with each other." That's a problem that YABT is trying to solve, both by providing its own resources to fill gaps and by coordinating information among existing organizations to improve coverage.

Viguria said programs like TIC Americas help individual entrepreneurs, but entrepreneurism has the potential to transform the entire region. "It's about competitiveness to us. Our young people need to think outside the box; they need to think ahead. We don't want our young people to create a business to only think about selling it to their neighbors or inside the community. They need to sell it in the global market. One of the requirements of TIC Americas is to have a Web site. If they have a Web site, anybody in the world can access their product or service. So they are already in the global market."

THE SEEDS ARE SPROUTING

All of this coordinated institutional investment complements the powerful dynamics of demographics, technology innovation, and globalization to lay the groundwork for a new, bottom-up model of economic development across the Young World, based on indigenous entrepreneurship. It has supercharged the incubation of new talent and new businesses in the same way that genetic modification of crops has supercharged agricultural production. The next chapter looks at the huge harvest of talent, innovation, and entrepreneurial energy that is about to ripen, even in parts of the world that have proven enormously challenging to economic development.

Because this brand of entrepreneurship has emerged directly from the same blend of youth and technology that gave birth to the global Net Generation, it exhibits some characteristics that are uniquely well-adapted to the conditions of the new global economy, as well as a spirit that is grounded in can-do Millennial optimism. In the pages ahead, we will hear their stories.

CHAPTER 3

YOUNG WORLD ENTREPRENEURSHIP IN ACTION

"I'd like to share a personal story, if you don't mind," said Yerutí Méndez, Director of Training and Technology for the Young Americas Business Trust, toward the conclusion of our interview. I had just asked whether she felt that entrepreneurship was realistically a path open to those at the bottom of the pyramid, or whether it was only an option for educated Young World elites.

"I'm from Paraguay, a very poor country, one of the most corrupt countries in the world," she said. "There was a time around 1997, during the financial crisis that affected Argentina, Paraguay, and Brazil, we were very . . ." Her voice wavered as she conjured up the memory. "My family was broke. At that point, my parents didn't even have the money for us to go to school. My mother was fighting cancer. We were in high school, and we couldn't even enroll. My brother said 'Okay, I'm going to start a company and I'll be able to pay for you to go to school.' And my parents said, 'No, you can't do that. You can't spend all the money we have on something that's not going to work.'

So the first reaction my parents had was that it wasn't an investment, it was something they would lose."

Yerutí's brother pressed on with his idea. He wrote his business plan, pulled the family's finances together, and got his company underway. "He started a company to print T-shirts, and after five months he was making profits," said Yerutí. "He was so motivated! We were going to school in the morning and working from four to ten at night because we needed to get the work done so we could eat and go to school.

"That was something that changed our family. Now, each member of my family has a business. It changed our life. We said, 'We can't be employees; we have to have something by ourselves.' And we are proud of that. It made our family have an income. Now we're helping more than 20 families to have a source of income. So yes, even the most poor people, if they believe in what they're doing, they can have a success story."

* * *

Yerutí's story is the traditional narrative of the individual entrepreneur: what used to be called the American Dream, but now belongs to the wider world. If the spread of entrepreneurship were the only driving theme in the rise of the Young World, it would still be a significant trend. Hope can change lives. Empowerment can transform communities. Enterprise can lift up entire nations.

That is a lot of potential resting on the shoulders of people like Yerutí and her family. Fortunately, in the age of a global Net Generation united by ubiquitous connectivity, entrepreneurism has become a borderless, collaborative endeavor with unprecedented resources available to shepherd great ideas into fruition. The drive, talent, and ambition of individual entrepreneurs can now be channeled and amplified through the coordinated efforts of individuals, governments, non-government organizations (NGOs), and grass-roots networks made possible by social collaboration and pervasive access to information.

THE DISTINCTIVE QUALITIES OF YOUNG WORLD ENTREPRENEURSHIP

The spread of mobile and network technology is introducing the billions in the Young World to the mindset of the global Net Generation, and more and more of these young people are looking to make an impact by creating organizations that succeed on both social and commercial terms. Their efforts are driving a swelling wave of information and communications technology (ICT)-based entrepreneurship, distinguished by six features that reflect the unique influence of the Net Generation norms (collaboration, global focus, sense of urgency, use of networked technologies, and so on) described in Chapter 1. Young World entrepreneurship:

1. Blends social and commercial objectives
2. Creatively aligns public, private, and NGO resources
3. Leverages communities and collaboration
4. Is well-adapted and sustainable in Young World environments
5. Embraces the globalization of the knowledge workforce
6. Solves systemic problems while meeting market needs

Each of these features enables the growth and spread of innovative ventures in areas where adverse conditions have made indigenous economic development nearly impossible in the past.

1. **Blends social and commercial objectives**. In low-income countries, the simple act of creating a business that employs others serves an important social purpose. However, the new generation of Young World entrepreneurs sees its mission in broader terms than that. Because they have a close and personal connection to the difficult conditions that prevail in their environments, their business ventures tend to put explicit discretionary effort behind social goals such as workforce development, community-building, local problem-solving, and civic society initiatives, even when they are primarily market-oriented. In fact, Young World entrepreneurs show a particular genius for finding market opportunities in developing solutions to social problems, incorporating the social aspect seamlessly into the DNA of their organizations.

2. **Creatively aligns public, private, and NGO resources**. In the past, government, private-sector corporations, and non-government organizations tended to pursue different and often contradictory paths in regards to commercial and social development, reflecting their different agendas. Young World entrepreneurs, working within the framework of private companies, NGOs, or even governments themselves, look for ways to bring those objectives into alignment by designing programs that satisfy multiple constituencies simultaneously. These efforts are effective because they recognize the legitimacy of the market goals of the private partners and appreciate the political complexities facing their public partners, rather than simply relying on good intentions and lofty ideals.

3. **Leverages communities and collaboration**. Young World entrepreneurs have built out entire platforms for knowledge sharing and collaboration based on everything from the simplest text-messaging features found on the most rudimentary mobile phones to the latest Web 2.0 technologies. For the generation that grew up alongside the Internet, this networked mode of organizing is the default, as opposed to the central command-and-control style that predominated in years past. As consumers, citizens, and entrepreneurs, they exploit the possibilities of these platforms by creating self-organized communities to reduce costs, deliver critical information, develop open source software solutions, share business practices, and build bridges across geographic and social divides.

4. **Is well-adapted and sustainable in Young World environments**. Young World entrepreneurs don't have the luxury of being extravagant in the design or marketing of their products. Their customers may have limited resources, but this makes them even more sophisticated and value-conscious. Consequently, successful Young World ventures make intensive use of the latest ICTs to drive down costs and carefully target their offerings with lean-and-mean precision. Then, once they are able to meet global standards of performance, they can leverage their process efficiency and relatively lower labor costs to compete effectively in high-income markets.

5. **Embraces the globalization of the knowledge work-force**. "Globalization" may be a dirty word in some quarters, but to Young World entrepreneurs, it spells opportunity. Young World ventures not only take into account the instant access to world markets afforded by networks and expanded connectivity, they also capitalize on the transnational fluidity of talent and what this means for the future of work. Employment relationships in the knowledge economy are evolving to the point where many knowledge-workers see themselves as self-contained entrepreneurs, their employers as clients and their workplace skills as a capital portfolio requiring constant attention and diversification. Young World entrepreneurs deliberately cultivate workplace cultures that attract and nurture the global creative class, and blend work and social activities in ways that represent significant departures from their countries' traditional workplace experiences.

6. **Solves systemic problems while meeting market needs**. Entrepreneurs in emerging or less-developed countries face challenges related to the underdeveloped physical and civic infrastructure. These range from unreliable power transmission to dishonest governments, poor access to capital and credit, a workforce that does not meet global employability standards, high-priced computers and Internet connections, a "brain drain" of educated expatriates, and unfair competition from foreign multinationals. Rather than wait for top-down, institutional responses to these problems, Young World entrepreneurs are filling the gaps in their own entrepreneurial ecosystem at multiple points, simultaneously, from the bottom up. They are building capacity, creating connections, solving problems, and becoming globally competitive in the knowledge economy—and making money doing so. Each new success reinforces the system as a whole, providing a model for others who would follow in their footsteps and providing reassurance to risk-averse creditors, partners, and customers.

Because we are so accustomed to the slow pace of top-down development through government programs, aid, foreign direct investment, and the arrival of established multinationals to signal the maturation of Young World markets, it can be difficult to perceive how this swarm of small-scale indigenous entrepreneurism is effecting such a massive and consequential transformation in parts of the world that are, frankly, easy to ignore if you are sitting in New York, London, or Tokyo. They are about to become much less easy to ignore.

The stories in this chapter look at a variety of organizations and individuals whose accomplishments are laying the groundwork for an explosion of bottom-up growth across the Young World, and whose achievements are inspiring others around the world. Rather than organize the examples along the lines of size (small-medium enterprise or global), mission (social or commercial), or region, I have deliberately created juxtapositions between small, community-focused efforts and burgeoning multinationals, between entrepreneurial ventures at the rugged frontiers of the global economy and those at its developed core, and between those launched by starry-eyed newcomers as compared to accomplished veteran entrepreneurs like dotcom pioneer Gunjan Sinha or Ghana's Herman Chinery-Hesse. The cases are examples of common problems facing the entrepreneurial ecosystem as a whole as well as stories of the individual projects of the entrepreneurs, and fall into these general categories:

- *Increasing Knowledge Economy Skills*. Indigenous entrepreneurs—social, commercial, and a blend of both—are actively engaging the young populations in their community to build everything from basic IT competency to the sophistication necessary to be employable in the global knowledge economy.
- *Building Connections*. Entrepreneurs are not only leveraging existing information networks and platforms like Facebook, Twitter, and the blogosphere, they are also building dedicated resources to spread knowledge, draw attention to local innovation, facilitate the mobility of talent, and promote the successes of Young World entrepreneurs around the globe.
- *Improving Conditions*. There is no shortage of problems in the Young World, from poverty to corruption to natural disasters. Young World entrepreneurs are applying their ingenuity, their tech skills, and their personal familiarity with local conditions to bring market-based and blended solutions to supplement—or supplant—the efforts of governments and international NGOs.

- *Reaching the Global Market.* Whether as inventors of new products, organizers of local markets, or developers of new content and services, Young World entrepreneurs are going directly to the global marketplace via the Internet, branded platforms, and the latest social computing tools.
- *Achieving Escape Velocity.* Young World entrepreneurship has produced a small but growing number of multinational knowledge economy companies that compete and win at the very highest levels of global business. India's Infosys is perhaps the best-known example, and it is charting a path that others will follow, even as it continues to innovate and define the terms of success in this arena.

Even within these categories, there is overlap in methodology and mission. The point of this mashup approach is to convey the overwhelming energy and diversity that I discovered while conducting this research. Despite a dour economy and omnipresent political uncertainty, the Young World is buzzing with new activity and new ideas. Billions of voices, many of them newly arrived on any stage larger than their village or town, are clamoring to be heard. I have tried, in the telling of these stories, to give pride of place to those voices.

INCREASING THE SKILLS OF THE KNOWLEDGE WORKFORCE

People are a necessary ingredient in knowledge economy development, but people by themselves are not sufficient. The knowledge economy requires people to understand how to use software and information tools, which can be complex, and to fathom the implicit rules and customs that govern their use in business. The always-on, always-connected digital culture of networks and social media takes some getting used to. As I have argued elsewhere,[1] it matters when— at what point in their development—people encounter information and communication technology. Because that experience is so powerful, it has the ability to shape perceptions and expectations that people bring with them to the world of work.

Falling prices and wider availability of computers, mobile devices, networks, and online services are helping to transform the world's

4.2 billion Millennials into a wired Net Generation of titanic proportions by exposing them to the wider world of information and digital culture. However, the tactical work of refining that familiarity into skillssuitable for work in the knowledge economy still depends largely on local education systems. Despite a lot of lip service from government ministers and plenty of outside assistance, most Young World education systems are too strapped for resources and too short of teachers with the right training to shoulder this burden.

Now a new generation of Young World entrepreneurs is helping to fill the gaps in workforce development for the knowledge economy. They are doing so by applying the new and distinctive methods described above, particularly by aligning corporate, government, and NGO resources and interests; leveraging global networks; addressing issues such as gender and class-based discrimination at the most local and personal levels; and finding ingenious ways of blending social and commercial objectives.

Young World social entrepreneurs like Paradigm Initiative Nigeria's 'Gbenga Sesan work opportunistically with government, NGOs, and corporate partners as part of a very deliberate strategy that connects the nuts-and-bolts of technology training, anti-cybercrime, and local business promotion to the much larger agenda of economic development. Halfway around the world, in the southern islands of the Philippines, Stephanie Caragos has found a way to marry the market goals of her commercial business with the social priorities of providing training, experience and employability skills to develop the local knowledge workforce. Bit by bit, these Young World social entrepreneurs are weaving a new narrative of success to replace the old visions of dependency and despair, and this, in turn, is attracting wider attention and resources.

Their small-scale successes not only directly help their communities by creating employment and wealth, they also provide role models for subsequent waves of entrepreneurs.

Bringing Knowledge Economy Skills to the Base of the Pyramid: Paradigm Initiative Nigeria

At age 32, 'Gbenga Sesan is already a veteran in the organizational efforts to broaden ICT-based opportunities for young people in his native Nigeria and across West Africa. His current organization, Paradigm Initiative Nigeria (PIN), a nonprofit that explores the space between technology and economic development for his country's youthful population, grew out of networks he first established in 2001.[2]

PIN partners with numerous organizations within and outside Nigeria to deliver bottom-up, solution-driven, and community-owned projects, especially in communities where ICT solutions can make an impact. The group is active in ICT and entrepreneurship training and mentoring for youth in the slums of Lagos, anti-cybercrime initiatives, and programs that raise awareness of the opportunities available to computer-literate young people. Today, it is a hub for NGOs, government, local businesses, multinationals, and individuals who share an interest in promoting the spread of tech skills and grassroots entrepreneurship.

The central role of NGOs is nothing new in Nigeria or elsewhere in the developing world, but PIN is part of a new wave of activity undertaken by indigenous organizations focused extensively or exclusively on using technology as both the means and the ends of economic development. Sesan himself works with everyone from Microsoft to the government of Nigeria to the United Nations, advocating for greater investments in ICT workforce development and creating connections that align the interests of large organizations with the needs of the local population. He served on the Nigerian Presidential Task Force on the Restructuring of the Nigerian Information Technology and Telecommunications sectors before he turned 30 and was Nigeria's first Information Technology Youth Ambassador.

Over the last several years, Sesan has seen the convergence of youth (nearly 45% of Nigeria's population is under the age of 15) and ICT reach critical mass. "We did a report in 2005 on youth and ICT in Nigeria. At the time we thought the growth was high, but it's been astronomical between then and now," he said. "There is still a digital divide: it's been slow for those at the lower end of the spectrum; it's been extremely fast for those at the higher end of the spectrum."

Sesan said there's a strong disconnect between the younger generation, who speak English and have access to online resources, and the older generation, particularly in the rural areas, who have never known technology and would probably not be interested in it. "Of course that's changing over the years, because Nigeria is a very young country. The younger population is larger, so the numbers are reducing."

He is guardedly optimistic about the prospects for closing the ICT skills gap in ways that provide Nigeria's young workforce with knowledge economy skills. "Poverty is very strongly linked to how they are able to beat the learning curve or the participation curve. I'm afraid it's going to be like that for a while, because many of the families at the bottom of the pyramid are still not able to afford the expensive training. Eventually, over maybe five to seven years, we are going to have a lot more projects giving them access via public facilities."

Government participation is critical to provide the resources to scale these training efforts across the length and breadth of Africa's most populous country. Sesan points to an initiative undertaken by the government of Nigeria to deploy community communication centers (CCCs), tapping the universal services fund, which is managed by the national telecom regulator. "Those CCCs are for those who can't afford to go to the training, so they can come to learn. Infrastructure wise, they are planning for that."

Unfortunately, government policy toward ICT-led growth is as consistent as Lagos's notoriously unreliable power grid. "The government has paid a lot of, if I may, lip service to the issue of software development," said Sesan. He cites the example of the government's commitment to set up the national software development institute by renovating a disused site in central Lagos. "A few months after that announcement was made, they changed the other way and said the facility would now be used for housing for Nigerians in the diaspora who are returning home. That gave everyone an idea of the priority that the government was giving to software development. Yes, there is a task force, but the committed resources were taken away without any thought."

The Nigerian ICT industry has another problem on its hands: Nigeria has become synonymous in the eyes of the West with cyber-crime, specifically a kind of e-mail fraud that encourages unwary victims to disclose personal information that allows the fraudsters access to bank accounts and credit information. This crime is actually described as "Nigerian Fraud" in the operating manuals of Interpol and other international law enforcement organizations. Its biggest victims, however, are the legitimate ICT businesses and consumers of Nigeria.

"If you search for Nigeria on the Internet, the first few things you'd find are related to 419, which is the section of the penal law in Nigeria which describes such activities," said Sesan with a tinge of exasperation in his voice. "Now, that is unfortunate for legitimate online businesses in Nigeria, because the first reaction of institutions that are supposed to serve us, e.g., financial platforms, is to have a negative attitude toward Nigeria. For example, PayPal will never allow you to register as a user if you have a Nigerian address. Amazon. com will not deliver goods to a Nigerian address. Some of them have even blacklisted Nigerian addresses and Nigerian credit cards, which in itself is putting a huge pillar between legitimate businesses and the opportunities they could have had access to."

Consequently, a lot of PIN's capacity-building activities are aimed at preventing cybercrime and raising public awareness about it. "One thing we're trying to work on is where we have these young people who have the [technology] skills, but are directing them in the wrong areas," said Sesan. "We bring them into a rehabilitation program where they are trained and taken through an internship process back into the formal economy, where they can [express] some of the value that we know they own."

PIN recently partnered with Microsoft on a major counter-cybercrime initiative. The Unlimited Potential Program's Internet Safety Initiative focused on Internet safety and brought together stakeholders from the public, private, NGO, and multinational communities. It was a year-long program that engaged at-risk youth with awareness events featuring prominent entertainers, free software, and outreach that outlined the opportunities of legitimate ICT as well as the risks of engaging in illicit activity.

The problem of cybercrime touches on another subject that has an impact on workforce development in Nigeria and, indeed, other traditional societies: the participation of women. "A lot more young men are interested in technology than women," observed Sesan, "and unfortunately this is another place where cybercrime has an effect, because the perception of technology among young women in Nigeria is affected by cybercrime. A lot of young women are staying off technology for that reason."

Surmounting the challenges posed by Nigeria's digital divide, infra-structure, reputation, and governance are worth the effort, according

THE WOMEN'S TECHNOLOGY EMPOWERMENT CENTER

The Women's Technology Empowerment Center (W.TEC)[3] is a Nigerian NGO working to empower girls and women socially and economically, using information and communication technologies. It was launched in January 2008 and runs a variety of programs throughout Nigeria and English-speaking Africa, mainly focused on basic Internet competency, blogs, and social media. Ore Somolu, W.TEC's executive director, says the organization runs the gamut from giving girls their first exposure to the online world to helping woman entrepreneurs learn the skills and tools to grow their businesses.

"Here in Nigeria, even though times are changing, it is still a very traditional society," Somolu said. "It is very rooted in old cultures and religion. So there are still certain ideas of what women should be doing and what women should aspire to, and what men can do and aspire to." For women, said Somolu, learning how to use technology, which is considered predominantly a male thing, is really liberating: "They can break the defined gender roles."

W.TEC's first project targeted women who work in NGOs and the nonprofit sector, because it was felt that, as these women work with lots of different communities, if they were empowered to use the different tools or adopt an ICT-friendly attitude, they would naturally pass this on to some of the clients with whom they work. Eventually they opened up the program to women from different backgrounds. "We taught them how to use blogs, wikis, and podcasts, and we taught them how to use social networking sites to form networks. Some set up blogs and Facebook groups for businesses they were running at the time or after the program was started, and they used that to promote their businesses."

to Sesan, because the prospect of growing the knowledge economy sector presents an irresistible opportunity to move the country onto a more sustainable path of economic development. "It annoys me every time I think that the whole development strategy for Nigeria is based on the price of crude oil. That is not a sustainable way to develop a country. Going forward, the young people who are engaged in technology platforms and active development services are going to be

Nigeria's future, once we realize that we don't only have to depend on natural resources."

To advance this vision, Sesan helped to promote a youth conference, BarCamp Nigeria—an online gathering to exchange ideas and share information—in April 2009, which attracted more than 150 participants worldwide. Sesan said that it was probably the first time that so many young people came together on the same platform to discuss the opportunity to provide socioeconomic leadership for the country focusing on the vast potential of ICT-led entrepreneurship, business creation, and workforce development around software design and delivery. "The model that seems to be working mostly at the moment is delivering applications and services to the local market, because we've got a West African market of almost 300 million. We have an African- and English-speaking Southern market that is extremely large in terms of developing economies. If you develop an application in Nigeria, it's almost immediately relevant across West Africa, in East Africa, across Southern Africa. If I sell a thousand applications at one dollar apiece, that's a lot better than waiting for the price of oil to increase, which I have no control over whatsoever.

"I believe, knowing the trends in Nigeria, once those things are in place, content is definitely not going to be a problem: People will take advantage of the infrastructure to create content, some of them on a voluntary basis, and some of them on a commercial basis, priced for the bottom of the pyramid. So there are huge opportunities for all those young people who are not focused on natural resources, but are focused on using technology platforms. The moment the institutions become more stable and they deliver more in terms of revenue, that will provide an alternative path for the country as a whole."

Providing World Class IT Services with Local Talent: LetITHelp (Philippines)

The Philippines has a vibrant, youthful, literate, and predominantly English-speaking population, a stable democracy, strategic location, cultural ties to Asia, Latin America, and the United States, and an economy that has been humming along at near double-digit growth rates for much of the decade. ICT penetration rates are high and increasing with the falling costs and increased quality of service.

Knowledge-economy business creation is spreading beyond the urban hub of Manila to the small towns and cities that dot the archipelago.

What has been missing in the Philippines is that final step of work-force development that refines the talent of young knowledge workers to the highest standards of the global economy. The shortage of truly capable workers is starting to create bottlenecks for businesses looking to move up the value chain and serve global as well as local customers. This is an area of focus for the government, the educational sector, and NGOs, but almost by definition, these institutions cannot provide what is really lacking: professional experience. Only the real work environment of an ICT business can provide firsthand exposure to real-world working conditions and the demands of global business that high-value work requires.

Stephanie Caragos is a prototypical Young World entrepreneur who saw an opportunity to align social and business needs, fill a gap in the knowledge economy entrepreneurial ecosystem, and grow her own commercial enterprise. Her story illustrates how the current generation of Young World entrepreneurs is not making a firm either-or choice between social and commercial goals, but instead devising practical for-profit business plans that incorporate strongly-felt personal and social values.

After graduating from Xavier University in the Philippines in 2000, Caragos and some friends decided to start up their own IT business developing financial management software in their community of Cagayan de Oro on the southern island of Mindanao. Some time later, she launched Syntactics Inc.,[4] a commercial Web and software development outsourcing company, with her old colleague, Wilfredo "Jun" Kaamino as Vice President and COO.

Syntactics is a provider of business services for the Web, including search engine optimization, application development, design, and integration, and has won several Philippine business awards. Caragos says that the company does about half of its business domestically and half for overseas outsourcing customers. As with all such businesses, the quality and competitiveness of its services depends on the talent of its developers. Local colleges and technical training schools were putting out a steady stream of graduates with IT degrees or certificates, but Caragos observed that these young people were having difficulty finding work in their field because their preparation fell just short of the standards required by firms that aspired to global competitiveness, including Syntactics.

"We saw that in our city of Cagayan de Oro, there weren't any IT businesses that could provide the careers that a lot of kids were studying for," she said when we spoke in the summer of 2009. "A lot of the students do not come from well-off backgrounds. We started seeing that there were a lot of companies who wouldn't accept graduates for that reason, and also because they didn't have enough experience. It's easy to choose somebody who graduated from a high-end college compared to someone who graduated from somewhere not so known. They always pick the higher-end college. So we were seeing that there was underemployment for these kids. They weren't getting the jobs that they were supposed to have, they didn't get the right opportunities for them to live their dreams and to believe in themselves."

In 2008, Caragos and Kaamino spun off a "social enterprise" from their main Syntactics business with the goal of providing training, experience, and mentoring to this segment of the young workforce. They called the organization LetITHelp, and they recruited their first class of 15 in the spring of 2008. LetITHelp is organized as a non-profit in that it can accept grants and ordinations, partner with NGOs that promote capacity-building, and provide transparent accounting to donors through financial and social impact reports. However, it is intimately connected with the commercial business, and the young trainees work side-by-side with the full-time staff in a professional environment.

Caragos says the response has been tremendous. "The trainees know that they are being taught by really good professional teachers and practitioners. They are getting the training from one of the best IT companies in Mindanao. And there's been a lot of confidence in what they can do and how they believe in themselves. So right now, yes, it's still commercial in a sense, but it is more of a social enterprise, because at LetITHelp, we want to make sure that they do need the job and they will be the kind of people that help other people in the end."

The connection between personal and professional development is at the heart of the LetITHelp project, and is something which distinguishes it from a more run-of-the-mill apprenticeship program. Trainees are immediately given a salary, which provides them with a measure of financial independence and self-confidence.

"Aside from the financial support that we give them through salaries, we provide activities and training to make it more holistic. They get retreats, they get lectures and seminars in how to become better people, seminars in sales, seminars in physical grooming and all that," said Caragos. "Some people might think it crazy, that those are basics, that we shouldn't be including stuff like that, but then these kids never had the opportunity to get these kinds of life-training seminars. We 're talking about graduates from IT programs who are about 19 years old, 20 years old, who didn't have much opportunity to learn these things. We encourage them to be more concerned about other people around them and not just themselves, and remind them that they got into the program first and foremost because they have the skills and the potential, but [also] because they have the opportunity and the potential to help others. They know that their vision and their goal is to become someone that can help others as well."

Caragos says that the LetITHelp program also provides opportunities to enhance their English language skills—a prerequisite to employment in global-facing businesses—and to learn aspects of business and financial management, including how to put together budgets and resources for IT development projects. "We're trying to let them realize that through employment and profession and career, they can move forward. They are able to sustain their family and be able to help their family financially. In that way they can also help their siblings finish college and get good educations. When their other siblings get a good education, they are able to augment their families' status. In the Philippine culture, when somebody leaves home, they start helping their relatives as well. It becomes a domino effect for everybody else."

This very intense and social approach to training has created a talent pipeline not only for the commercial venture, Syntactics, but also for other IT service providers in the area. Caragos networks with other companies around the Philippines to keep tabs on workforce development issues. She is also part of ysei.org, a global network of knowledge economy social entrepreneurs, and has gained a lot of recognition for herself and her business as a result of the visible success of LetITHelp.

"Having a social enterprise opens up [business opportunities]," Caragos explained. "Our customers learn how [our trainees] are setting up on their own feet, and becoming independent, and helping other people. We get appreciated more. Instead of saying 'this is our service, this is our fee,' we tell them this is our service, this is what we can do for you, and these are the people who are actually working for you. It gives them a better sense of fulfillment knowing that they are able to get the service that they need, and at the same time, help other people. It is good. Sometimes when clients come and visit our office, we introduce them to this staff member, or that trainee that we're working with on their projects, and they get the feeling that they were able to touch the lives of other people [in addition to] getting a professional service."

Over the next three to five years, Caragos hopes to ramp up both sides of her business. LetITHelp expects to induct a new class of 30–50 trainees in late 2009, and as revenues grow, Caragos said she is interested in expanding into a more formal training institute that integrates classroom learning, discussions, seminars, and guest speakers into the existing program.

"Within the five years, one of our goals is to provide opportunities for at least 200 youth," Caragos said. "Looking at it in a social impact point of view, with those 200 people we will be able to help at least 1,000 people, because the average family size here in the Philippines is five. It becomes a cascading effect. Basically that's the concept, that's our dream, and we hope to grow further."

BUILDING CONNECTIONS

In today's interconnected world, entrepreneurship is a profoundly connected and collaborative endeavor. Social computing technology, especially social networks, blogs, and online communities, brings entrepreneurs together across geographic and cultural distances to share knowledge, gain attention for their projects, find people to collaborate with, and get the kind of positive social reinforcement that keeps you going through 20-hour days and the hard work of setting up a business. The growth and spread of these social networks is helping to catalyze the potential seeded by capacity-building investments, bringing people into connect with ideas, opportunities, and markets that can push their business plans to the next level.

These networks also foster a kind of micro-entrepreneurship wherein knowledge professionals take ownership of their careers, seeing employment as a series of client engagements rather than as the more formal and permanent arrangement common in the 20th century. Dan Rasmus and I, in our book *Listening to the Future*, call this the Freelance Planet scenario, wherein knowledge nomads use social networks the way Tarzan uses vines, swinging from job to job, partnering up around specific opportunities, then dispersing again into the talent jungle. Although they are not necessarily seeking to start businesses that create employment for others, the denizens of Freelance Planet behave like entrepreneurs and benefit from the same apparatus of social networks and information resources.[5]

Creating collaborative spaces for entrepreneurs and global knowledge workers is itself the focus of entrepreneurial activity. Some of the most energetic and successful innovators I spoke to are working on platforms designed to create more opportunities for Young World talent, whether their goal is to build a business or promote their own careers.

Reinventing the Recruitment Process for the Global Knowledge Economy: Brave New Talent (United Kingdom)

Lucian Tarnowski, 26, has modest goals for his London-based startup, Brave New Talent.[6] He wants to redefine the relationship between employers and job-seekers and reinvent the recruitment process to fit the realities of the global talent market in an era of pervasive social media. When we spoke in April, 2009, he was also helping to organize a conference to bring together more than 1000 young leaders from 192 countries. (The event, called "One Young World," took place in February, 2010 and was, by all accounts, a great success.) Brave New Talent provides companies with a way to get involved in the workforce development process earlier, helping target the companies' efforts toward developing the skills of the people most likely to wind up in their employ. It's a model that leverages the advantages of social media and the entrepreneurial approach that NetGeners are taking toward their careers. Tarnowski believes it has the potential to bring Young World talent into the global knowledge economy much more rapidly by helping to close one of the biggest remaining gaps: employability.

Tarnowski himself is serious and passionate about his business, but quite obviously enjoys being 26, dapper, and successful, as a cursory glance at his Twitter feed reveals. I caught up with him in the early evening as he was preparing to head out for a night on the town.

"My big goal with Brave New Talent is to show employers all those individuals who want to work for them, the whole community of people that want to work for them, before they apply," he enthused, in the polished tones of someone who has been making this pitch before serious people with large sums of money to invest. "Right now, an employer only knows who wants to work for them after they've received their application. They have rough numbers, but they don't know the faces and the individuals or anything about them. Brave New Talent shows them who those individuals are, which gives employers a unique opportunity to recruit earlier, the opportunity to build a stronger employer brand, and to network and engage."

Tarnowski explained his vision of using the Facebook platform to bring employers and job-seekers together early in the recruitment process, so that each could spend some time learning about the other before entering into a more formal commitment. His company's use of Facebook Connect allows people to create a separate Facebook profile for job searching ("minus all the pictures from last weekend down at the pub"), and associate it with employer-created sites to indicate interest in potential opportunities. Employers learn a little bit about the potential applicants as individuals, and a lot about the way they are perceived in the talent marketplace through the aggregate type of applicant they attract. That information not only helps them target and fine-tune their recruitment efforts, but also allows them to begin a pre-orientation for promising recruits much earlier in the process than before.

What this means, says Tarnowski, is that the traditional process of recruitment and selection gets turned on its head. "This idea that recruitment is there to create as wide a funnel as possible and narrow that down to the best candidates is completely wrong in my view. [In the new global talent market] it's all about getting as *few* of the *right* candidates as possible. I think the future of recruitment is all around encouraging the *de-selection* of candidates, of correct matching, basically."

Like Stephanie Caragos, Tarnowski is deeply concerned with the issue of "employability skills"—that is, the kind of awareness and polish that comes from familiarity with professional work environments: how to communicate appropriately with co-workers and customers; how to express oneself in writing; how to find, apply, and assess information; how to manage and be managed in a knowledge workplace. These kinds of skills are part and parcel of the higher education system in mature economies—where polish and professionalism indeed too often substitute for deep subject-matter knowledge—but they are not necessarily prevalent in educational environments that rely on old techniques of rote learning, memorization, and standardized testing, which are common in many emerging economies. Consequently, even those fortunate and dedicated enough to have completed post high-school education programs and intensive training curricula may still not be suitable for better-paid, more dignified, and creative jobs in the global knowledge economy.

Tarnowski sees an opportunity to bridge that gap for Young World talent and the world-class companies who need that talent to compete. The global reach of the Internet means that the pool of potential talent is no longer limited to the nearby community or even the domestic workforce, but can extend to anyone with skills and interest anywhere in the world.

Though his company is based in the United Kingdom, deep in the heart of the Old World, his plans extend immediately to the global market, especially those parts of the Young World where talented young people are looking for opportunities in the global knowledge economy. "I've always had a global outlook," he explained, noting that his father was an India expert and that he, Lucian, had been a Next Generation India Board member for the UK Indian Business Council following his graduation from university. "Not a bone in my body would want a U.K.-only company, no matter how big that company could be in the U.K. It's always been my goal from the very beginning to create a company that could scale globally. So that's why from the start I developed the rather strange idea of setting up an office in the U.K. and India."

Employability is a big problem in many developing countries, including India, he noted, citing a recent study by the trade association NASSCOM showing that a large percentage of university graduates lack the professional-level skills that meet global standards. "That means the Indian education system is failing the vast majority of its students. That's why we've got this massive movement of entrepreneurs. Every second entrepreneur in India is an education entrepreneur. I think the same problem exists across developing economies. It's employability that's the issue, not raw talent. Talent is universal and could come from anywhere. In India there's a huge amount of, you could call them unpolished gems, rough diamonds. If they are polished, by adding employability skills, suddenly they have tremendous value.

"My ambition here is to innovate the education sector and employ-ability market by allowing employers to be able to see the people who want to work for them, and therefore train them while they are still at university and, more importantly, off the payroll. It's a kind of 'virtual internship,' or virtual online academies around each employer. If we can build a community around each employer, we can allow that employer to train that community and use the response to the training as a way to recruit. It is a better, more informed way to recruit, over and above the CV, potentially leading to an interview."

Social media presents the ideal platform because it is the techno-logical representation of the Net Generation worldview: spontaneous, personalized, informal, entertaining, and bristling with opportunities to connect to people and information. Companies can use social plat-forms like Facebook to engage young job candidates where they live and leverage all the pre-existing social capital that comes with those platforms to jumpstart the dialogue.

"I think that social media is a phenomenal tool for engagement, and it can be a phenomenal tool for education as well, if it can be focused and targeted and given a purpose," says Tarnowski. "In my view, the real power of the Internet is to give employers a reason to get involved, because right now, the exponential pace of change that's happening in industry on a daily basis is far faster than the education system globally is able to keep up with. The gap between education and industry is widening on a daily basis. Social media is an incred-ibly powerful tool for communication as well as for education. It can provide the tools necessary and the engagement platform from which individuals can get better employability skills. Obviously, I've got high hopes for social media."

Like many tech-based entrepreneurial ventures launched by Net Geners, Brave New Talent tethers a noble social purpose—education and workforce development—to pure red-meat capitalism. The company wants to make a global market in talent in the same way that eBay makes a global market in stuff, with all the profitable upside that entails. At the same time, Tarnowski is passionately and sincerely committed to the empowerment of global youth, as evidenced by his related venture, One Young World,[7] which he is co-sponsoring alongside Kate Robertson and David Jones, the Chairman and CEO, respectively, of Euro RSGC Worldwide. It was getting late in the evening, but Tarnowski would not let me go until he told me about this.

"We're getting together over a thousand of the brightest young leaders, born 1984–1986, from every country in the world. So we've got 192 countries participating, every country that's recognized by the UN, and we're using social media to gather these people. I may be biased, but I think it is the most ambitious use of social media for the youth leadership cause globally. Perhaps it's even the most ambitious global use of social media in the biggest way ever. This is a global campaign to find future leaders."

One Young World's goal is to bring these young leaders to London for a leadership summit on February 8, 2010, and give them a platform with which their voices can be heard. Former UN Secretary General Kofi Annan, musician and philanthropist Bob Geldof, and Archbishop Desmond Tutu, all Nobel Peace Prize winners, are among the international luminaries involved in the event.

"Brave New Talent's role in this is to lead the social media outreach, lead the snowball viral effect, getting young people putting themselves forward as delegates," says Tarnowski. "Our goal is to get proportionate representation [according to population]. For developing economies, particularly China and India and Pakistan, it would be the first time in the history of those countries that they would have their population fully represented at a global event. Obviously that gets them really excited.

"We're getting people to create a profile on Brave New Talent, firing the search through our social media outreach." Candidates then gather as many votes as they can from their friends and their network. "It becomes a huge democratically selected group . . . When we sit down in February, democratic and proportionately-selected young leaders will have a response to [the climate change conference in] Copenhagen and other world forums, and no matter what that response is, it is of quite significant authority, as a youth voice. So the idea is to give young people a platform with which they can develop their leadership skills, make their voices heard, and through this network, encourage youth leadership at a younger age."

Tarnowski's idealistic commitment to the concept of One Young World is probably not entirely unrelated to the marketing opportunities this presents for his thematically-related startup, or to his own ambitions to emerge as a youth leader and global talent advocate. And that's okay. Part of the unique genius of Young World entrepreneurship in the Internet age is the ability to blend the social, the commercial, the personal, and the public in interesting ways that don't contradict one another or connote nefarious hidden agendas. The gaps he has identified in the global skills and recruitment process are real, and his solutions, whether or not they succeed, cleverly leverage new technology and the rising aspirations of the global NetGen to build necessary connections between Young World talent and opportunities in the worldwide knowledge economy.

Pooling Global Resources to Support Indigenous Entrepreneurship: Silicon India (United States/India)

One factor that has crippled knowledge economy entrepreneurship in emerging economies is brain drain. For the past half-century or more, many of the most talented and ambitious Indians, Chinese, Africans, South Asians, and Latin Americans left their homes to seek opportunities in the United States, Europe, and elsewhere overseas. In many cases, diaspora communities do quite well in terms of achievement and income. In the United States, for example, 58% of Indian-Americans have a college degree, compared to 27% of the general population; consequently, their median household income is $14,000 more per year than the average American family.[8] Even immigrants in nonprofessional occupations benefit from the higher pay scales and stronger currencies of developed countries; remitted wages from overseas workers constitute a significant component of foreign earnings for many countries, notably the Philippines, Pakistan, and Mexico. This creates strong incentives to leave home, stay in prosperous host countries, and raise families where opportunities are thick on the ground.

Despite popular attitudes to the contrary, host countries benefit as much or more as the immigrants themselves from the global migration of talent. Developing countries spend scarce resources educating and training their best and brightest, only to see those investments take flight when doctors, engineers, and other top talent desperately needed at home decide to chase higher incomes and better living standards by working abroad. Even large amounts of economic remittances do not compensate for the absence of people whose skills, knowledge, and positive example could contribute enormously to the development of indigenous capacity and local innovation.

The emergence of pervasive global networks goes a long way toward solving this problem by enabling the free flow of knowledge and resources between diaspora communities and the homeland. Technologies like Skype, which provide free voice and video communication over the Internet, and text-based tools like Twitter help knit together families and communities across the expanse of distance. This provides emotional comfort for individuals living far from their familiar environments. It also creates—and most importantly, preserves— the social capital that is the strength of so many of these communities and cultures.

This has important implications for global entrepreneurship. Not only can people keep in personal touch with distant family through voice, e-mail, photos, and video, but communities of young entrepreneurs can share information, make connections, find resources, farm out work, and trade business tips with well-established compatriots at home and abroad.

Now the brain drain is starting to reverse. The diasporas are returning home, as their Young World homelands become more politically stable, economically promising, and well-connected to the global knowledge economy. Increasingly, the convenience of networks goes both ways: former expatriates who return to their countries of ancestral origin can take advantage of emerging opportunities and improvements in living conditions while still keeping up ties with the economic and social relationships they formed in the United States, the United Kingdom, or wherever they had previously resided.

Providing resources for this growing community of transnational talent is fertile ground for knowledge economy entrepreneurs— especially those who bring ready-made familiarity with the cultures and the communities they aim to serve. Social networks such as Facebook and LinkedIn demonstrate the value of the concept, providing easy ways to manage relationships with large numbers of people in a bunch of different locations. Relatively simple from a technology standpoint, the sticky value of these sites is how they conjure up a framework of trust and social capital, where participants feel comfortable presenting a view of themselves through their personal profiles and sharing information, status updates, media clips, and miscellanea with their community of friends and associates.

The success of general social networking platforms has recently triggered an explosion in sites with similar features that target very specific social, professional, or psychographic audience segments. Communities of practice for entrepreneurs and freelance knowledge workers who can share tips, leads, ideas, and contacts with one another instantly, anywhere and anytime, constitute one of the big growth areas. They also provide connective tissue that can unite successful expatriates from Young World diasporas with the rising talent in their home countries, building strong partnerships based on the trust of ancient kinship ties and the instrumental value of up-to-the-minute business knowledge. This kind of know-how, previously at a premium in information-poor homelands, is now literally at the fingertips of any Young World entrepreneur who can access the right networks and channels.

SiliconIndia is a burgeoning social network based in the United States but aimed at persons of Indian origin (PIOs, in the parlance of the community) in India and around the world. It positions itself as "India's professional networking portal" and features knowledge, advice, job referrals, career development resources, and informal, firsthand information about employers and opportunities. It also aggregates news, lifestyle information, real estate and classified listings, and helpful tips for job seekers, students, and entrepreneurs on subjects like relocating, finding funding, shopping for internships, mentoring, and continuing education. As of August 2009, the site claimed more than 2 million members, with more than 50,000 new members joining each week.[9]

If SiliconIndia seems to target the market of Indian national and expatriate knowledge entrepreneurs with laser precision, perhaps that is because it is the brainchild of Gunjan Sinha, a quintessential Indian-expatriate knowledge entrepreneur. Sinha made his mark, and part of his fortune, by launching an early search engine, WhoWhere? in 1995, and then selling it to Lycos during the heyday of the dotcom mania. He parleyed that into several new ventures, including eGain and Metricstream, and has become a fixture on the boards of new media and net-based ventures in Silicon Valley.

I spoke with Sinha, a U.S. citizen who makes his home in northern California, in June 2009. He said he has been getting a lot of requests from people to help them with ideas, entrepreneurship, and general career advice. "More and more people started seeing entrepreneurship as a viable career option in India," he explained.

Sinha observed the success of The Indus Entrepreneur (TIE), a business roundtable set up in 1993 to support PIOs starting businesses in Silicon Valley primarily through conferences, local chapter meetings, and events. The organization eventually spread worldwide. Around 2000, Sinha decided to take the same kind of strategy online, and went into partnership with SiliconIndia, which was at that time a business magazine for IT executives.

"My basic vision was to create an online platform to connect the content, the community, the knowledge and information, and the network it takes to be able to create companies and entrepreneurial careers," Sinha explained. "SiliconIndia is a place for people who are interested in integration and creating *the next*, whether within the four walls of a top corporation, or if they want to start their next venture, or they want to join a start-up."

In the decades following independence, India's government was indifferent if not hostile to business creation. The regulatory environment, including the notorious "License Raj," made it costly, complicated, and time-consuming to get even simple businesses off the ground, leading many aspiring entrepreneurs to leave the country to follow their dreams. But now, Sinha believes things are starting to change.

"There is already a move in that direction with the liberalization of the country," he said. "People are getting in contact with other very successful entrepreneurs, so they are seeing that it's not impossible to create something and make something happen. A lot of this is about seeing success close by, because if you can see it, then you can feel it, [and then] you can do it. So we've seen definitely a rise of entrepreneurship in India and it's a trend which is only going to accelerate over the next decade or so."

Though SiliconIndia has had success attracting India's young urban elite, Sinha is most excited about the huge reservoir of talent and energy currently languishing at the bottom of the economic pyramid, including the more than 750 million people who live in rural communities that are only now getting hooked up to the global information grid.

"Part of the opportunity here is to create a talent development platform for both the haves and the have-nots," he explained. "You want to bridge the distance divide as far as possible. We want to draw upon those people. If you think about it, India has a billion entrepreneurs, because most of the people do not have a job and they don't work in the structured economy. They work by themselves; many of these people make under two dollars a day but they are fending for themselves. So how do you help those people as part of the long-term vision? How do I take somebody who makes two dollars a day and convert them into making twenty dollars a day? That's a tenfold increase in their earning potential, and is as much a success story as taking somebody who is working in a big multinational and helping them achieve a large IPO."

Sinha believes the members of the diaspora, like himself, have an important role to play in shepherding India's wealth of human capital into an asset in the global knowledge economy. For years, metropolitan India was indifferent to its diaspora. Harvard Business School professor Tarun Khanna, in his 2008 book *Billions of Entrepreneurs*, describes the policy of the Indian government toward Non-Resident Indians (NRIs) as one of dismissal and neglect. "Until recently, as hard as it was for an Indian within India to conduct business, purchase property, or even volunteer time or expertise to any cause, it was even harder for an NRI. Not until 2003, a decade after India launched its economic reforms, did the government create a Persons of Indian Origin policy, which extended benefits and concessions to ethnic Indians worldwide."[10]

Sinha, with his firsthand perspective, sees improvements in the relationship between the diaspora and the community within India, especially along the lines of business development. "There is more openness to taking ideas and views not just from people within India, but from both the diaspora community and from people from outside the Indian diaspora. So there is definitely much more influence which we exercise now than we did ever before."

Sinha says the Internet in general and social computing applications in particular are creating a forum for collaboration between the overseas community and people within the country, bringing about a potent blend of talent and ideas.

"If you look at what is happening here in Silicon Valley and what is happening in India, SiliconIndia is a way to create cross border collaboration across the globe," Sinha explained. "There is diffusion of ideas, and people are taking up things from each other which they would not have otherwise seen, if you saw these things as silos."

He says there have been a lot of people who got jobs and internships and have been recruited into different companies through his and other social networking platforms. "They have connected with people for nonprofit or social causes, through the groups and communities. That happens all day long. So many communities have members who are residing in the United States, in India, in a small village." By enabling constant, rich communication, the distances separating those branches of the community diminish, and the social ties of common purpose and heritage reassert themselves.

This has tremendous implications for integrating the hundreds of million people who live in rural India into the mainstream of the information age, despite the severe conditions of poverty that currently prevail. Again, we find that a social goal—closing the rural/urban digital divide—is very much at the forefront of this commercial entrepreneur's mission, and intimately tied to the service his company has developed.

"How do you bring in people who are earning less than two dollars a day into the whole of this network?" Sinha asked. "How do you do that and how do you change their lives? That is the big problem. I mean, think about it. Out of a billion people in India, 800 million people are below the poverty line. It is a huge number. The techniques of microfinance are only one part of the equation. How do you tie concepts of microfinance and entrepreneurial coaching so that a fisherwoman in small town is able to grow her income from two dollars a day to twenty dollars a day? How do you do that by leveraging a blogging platform and real-time networking and all of that stuff?"

Ultimately, Sinha believes that the power of bottom-up, collaborative entrepreneurship, facilitated by technology, offers the best hope of solving the challenging economic-development problems that have frustrated politicians, scholars, foreign aid institutions, and well-meaning experts. "There are a lot of social problems which these million minds can solve together. I call it a purpose-based network. Education and entrepreneurship is the one thing which can touch large numbers of people who do not have the premium education or entrepreneurship skills today. A lot of kids living in slums and rural India and so forth, they are not educated properly, because they do not understand the value of education. Many times they are financially not in a position to go for it. So I think this kind of network, through collaboration, can make that change happen and that will be very, very powerful."

IMPROVING CONDITIONS

Across the Young World, young entrepreneurs are looking to creative new ICT-based solutions that improve conditions for the billions of people living in poverty, uncertainty, and hardship. Unlike charities or traditional NGOs, these new entrepreneurial ventures combine social goals with commercial tactics, including partnerships with for-profit companies and market-oriented revenue models. These organizations tend to serve very low-income populations and therefore must keep their offerings simple, accessible, and affordable. In so doing, they are pioneering strategies for serving bottom-of-the-pyramid populations with top-of-the-line technology in ways that are profitable and sustainable.

Using Mobile Technology to Support Public Health: mPedigree (Ghana)

The World Health Organization estimates that as much as 30% of the medications distributed in the developing world to fight everything from malaria to AIDS are counterfeit, expired, or adulterated. Many are fatal, but even those that are not can cause other serious problems. Fake drugs compound the misery of people who desperately need medical help, lead to the evolution of drug-resistant strains of pathogens, and damage public confidence in the entire healthcare system. Who would see a doctor if there were a three-in-ten chance that the medication you receive could harm or kill you?

In 2007, Bright Simons, a young tech-savvy public policy researcher from Ghana, looked at this problem and wondered how ICTs could play a role in reassuring consumers about the medications they receive. He observed the rapid spread of mobile telephony throughout West Africa: Ghana had over 8.7 million mobile phone subscribers as of May 2008.[11] With a penetration rate approaching 50%, Ghana is a country where most citizens have at least some access to a mobile phone, even if it is a phone rented out by the local cab driver or shopkeeper. Although most of the handsets tend to be basic, they all include SMS texting capabilities. Simons figured that it might be possible to leverage that channel to deliver critical information about drug purity at the point of distribution to the end-user, so that every patient could be sure that they were receiving authentic medication.

"I came up with a concept [of using mobile telephony for authenticating pharmaceuticals] because I had an interest in China at that point," Simons told me during a visit to the United States in the summer of 2009. "Outsourcing was a big issue, and one of the related issues with outsourcing was counterfeiting. We came across the topic of medicine and mobile phones, the use of mobile phones as an indicator of how private enterprise sometimes [devises solutions that can serve the needs of non-profits]. So the two things came to a head, and I decided that mobile phones could be used against counterfeiting."

He and his partners conceived of a system where each lot of medication was tagged with a unique authentication code behind a scratch-off panel to prevent tampering. Consumers would scratch off the coating, then send a text message with the authentication code to a central server. The server would compare the code against a master database of known medications and, within a moment, return a text message to the original sender either validating the authenticity or not.

The genius of this approach is that it inverts the traditional logic of regulation. Consumers have direct access to the information they need to determine the authenticity of their medication, without having to rely on the efforts of government regulators, customs officials, and other top-down authority figures to vouch for drug purity. The information, and accountability, flows directly from the supplier to the end-user, through the simplest of mechanisms. They began work on the project, called mPedigree, in 2008. Some of the initial partners drifted away, leaving Simons to refocus the team's efforts based on some important things they had learned from the early development process.

For example, early in the process, mPedigree encountered issues that led them to believe that a successful program would have to be regional in scope, because so many of the medications in the Ghanaian market originally came from neighboring countries. That meant engaging the combined support of all the pharmaceutical companies to maintain a comprehensive master database.

"It appeared that the drug makers were going to immediately lift up and implement our pilot, because they have a problem," Simons explained. But it turned out there were other considerations beyond the problem of counterfeiting. There were issues to do with the nature and balance of the market, which was regional. There were issues to do with regulation, which were not always aligned with anti-counterfeiting. It soon became clear that the problem was complex enough to require the involvement, or at least the attention, of the government.

"When the pilot ended around April 2008 in Ghana, we began to assess on two fronts," said Simons. "One was to create a global platform, because we knew eventually it would have to be a global solution. Two, we had engage government in Ghana as a way of learning how to do it in other countries."

Part of the government's role was to secure a nationwide emergency exchange number and make sure it was well-publicized, so people would not be fooled or confused by counterfeiters sending out false authentication over their own bogus systems. Simons compared it to the 911 emergency dispatch system in the United States. "In the United States, no one wonders, you just call 911. If you have six other numbers, you might call someone who claims to be the police, but turns out to be burglars."

The government was needed to coordinate across the various telecom providers throughout Ghana and the region to make sure that the number was the same everywhere, regardless of the network or the location of the individual caller. Unfortunately, elections in Ghana brought a new government to power in the middle of the implementation, and mPedigree had to re-establish relations with a whole new cast of characters.

The experience helped prepare the organization for greater challenges elsewhere in the region and the developed world. The lessons Simons and his team learned are consistent with the emerging practices of Young World entrepreneurs around the globe.

"For two years we've been in Ghana. We've learned how to find the loopholes, we've learned how to plug them," said Simons. "We've found a suitable technology. What started out as a business is now a public-private partnership. We realized that partnership is fundamental; partnership is necessary. We acquired some skills. When we got to Nigeria, we got the same traction that we had in Ghana. We got to Rwanda. In Rwanda, we had our best bet, because the president himself wanted get something done in that country. So Rwanda happened very fast."

mPedigree was able to scale so broadly and so quickly because of its technology model. "The model works because it is virtual," Simons explained. "I don't need to set up data centers in every country. All I need is my data center in Ghana, and local partner[s] in any country that I want to go to. That way, you can you buy medicine [anywhere], you scratch the panel, you SMS the code, which is issued by the [local] telecom partner. That code goes via the Internet to our data center in Ghana, and you get a response nearly right away. It could be under two seconds."

Before long, the elephant of a different continent loomed large on mPedigree's radar. "We realized that for us to get to the kind of scale [and demonstrate] that is not really something that we just do for show, but is actually going to change the way they manage quality of service, we had to go to India, because that's where the size is. They are the largest drug market in the developing world. India produces a lot of its own generic drugs that are sold around the world. Also, India is the largest source of counterfeit medicines in the world. It's even bigger than China."

In India, Simons talked to the Tata Group, India's largest and oldest multinational conglomerate. "The person who owns Tata is a very social-entrepreneurial kind of person," said Simons. "His business has social dimensions to it. So Tata was a very good natural partner. We [are pursuing our strategy] with the contribution of Indian industry, trying to find a common understanding with them about how to do this, and also the Indian ministry of Corporate Affairs, which is the government's think tank, essentially."

Having learned the lessons of forging partnerships and aligning interests from its experiences in Africa, the organization brought those skills to bear in its new markets. Simons says he is hopeful that this and other initiatives the group is pursuing in places like the Philippines will quickly pay off and begin to close the net around the problem of global drug counterfeiting.

Improving Government through Social Entrepreneurship: GovLoop (United States)

One of the big tasks ahead for the global Net Generation is to make government more transparent, honest, and effective. Young World countries tend to be particularly poorly served by their governments, where corruption, cronyism, over-regulation, and inefficiency are endemic problems that strangle economic development and constrain personal freedom. Entrepreneurial ventures, public-private-NGO partnerships, and community-based technology solutions may prove a viable way to deliver the kinds of services typically associated with government, in a much more accountable and straightforward way. In the previous example, mPedigree managed to create an entrepreneurial, market-based solution for an important government function—regulation and enforcement of the authenticity of medications—that governments in the affected regions could not perform using the ordinary methods.

But the reinvention of government in the digital age is not just an issue for the dysfunctional and corrupt. Even the generally honest and productive governments of the developed world could use the help of social technology and information-sharing to perform their missions at lower cost to taxpayers.

Government work is not typically seen as a venue for entrepreneurism. However, civic-minded Millennials are finding ways to

innovate and create process efficiencies using networks and technologies, even if the management structures of the existing bureaucracy are not set up to accommodate them. One organization,
started by an entrepreneurial young government employee in the
United States as a sideline to his day job, illustrates how members of
the global Net Generation can apply Young World entrepreneurial
approaches even in the midst of one of the most hierarchical and
compartmentalized organizations on the face of the earth: the U.S.
government.

Steve Ressler joined the U.S. Department of Homeland Security
(DHS) after graduate school in 2004. He began reaching out to like-
minded young people through Young Government Leaders, a program
he founded with a friend over a few beers in a Washington, D.C. bar,
which eventually grew to encompass more than 2,000 federal, state
and local government workers across the United States.

In 2008, Ressler took the Young Government Leaders concept
online with a social network called GovLoop,[12] designed to facilitate
conversations across organizational boundaries to promote innovation
and share best practices. Ressler built the site using the Ning social
network development platform and administers it himself, with the
assistance of several volunteer moderators.

GovLoop features a news page, member blogs, community forums,
a wiki, and technology to integrate with other services such as Twitter
and Digg. The technical capabilities are up to date, but not cutting
edge, and are meant to be accessible to anyone with a passing familiarity with Facebook or LinkedIn. Membership is loosely limited to
government workers at all levels, plus academics, policy experts, and
what Ressler calls "good contractors" (the ones who aren't trying to
sell something).

"At first, people were asking themselves why they need to join
another social network," said Ressler. "Then they saw the rich
dialogues, the blogs, the events we were hosting on the site, and eventually it began to pick up steam."

Growth was slow and steady for the first six months, but in the
first half of 2009, the site mushroomed to a user base of more than
12,000, including growing numbers from outside the Beltway and
beyond U.S. borders. Member blogs have become the top feature of
the increasingly content-rich site, as government workers are able to

find an audience that appreciates the expertise they bring to public administration.

GovLoop has gained visibility as its user base has increased. In the age of Obama, Ressler says more and more foreign governments are looking to the United States for leadership on implementing Government 2.0 programs, and increasing numbers of GovLoop users are from places like Canada, Australia, the United Kingdom, and Germany.

Ressler believes that the main benefit of GovLoop is that it provides a channel for the rapid dissemination of best practices, so that people in various roles across the spectrum of government agencies don't have to re-invent the wheel when it comes to common tasks.

For example, Ressler cited the case of the City Investigator for the city of San Francisco, who was trying to implement a social media policy to improve outreach and communications. Rather than start from scratch, the investigator connected with someone in the state of Massachusetts, where they already had a mature and well-developed program, got all the information, and wrote the policy in a day instead of a week.

In another case, GovLoop helped an HR officer in the Department of Health and Human Services quickly obtain comparable pay and benefits scales from other agencies. The ability to connect directly through social media saved days or weeks of back-and-forth through standard bureaucratic channels.

"What's cool about government is that we're not competitors. So if I do something valuable at the Environmental Protection Agency, I can share that with colleagues in DHS, in the City of New York, in the State of Washington," said Ressler. "GovLoop exists to enable those peer-to-peer interactions, with the simple mission of improving government."

Crowdsourcing Crisis Response: Ushahidi (Kenya/Africa)

Natural disasters. Epidemics. Rigged elections. Ethnic violence. These are the Young World issues that most frequently capture the attention of the media, and thus the public, in high income countries. And while selective, sensationalistic reporting tends to skew perceptions, these types of problems are unfortunately still all too common in parts of the world that are the least equipped to respond to them.

One of the biggest problems in crisis response is the lack of current, good quality information about what's happening on the ground. Without a strategic view of the situation, organizations can err when deploying resources, or have trouble locating the multiple flashpoints that are causing the problems. These mistakes can cost lives and compound the negative effects, put others in needless risk, or escalate an already tense situation. In poorer regions, centrally managed crisis response, whether from the government or from outside organizations, has even fewer resources and weaker capabilities, compounding the stakes that hinge on every decision. And then there are those cases where the authorities themselves *are* the crisis, and count on a climate of information blackout to do their dirty work.

The advent of mobile communications and social networking technology fundamentally changes the dynamic of crisis response and information flow. In 2009, for example, we saw a determined group of Iranians take to the social media networks—primarily Facebook and Twitter—to make the world aware of the problems with their national elections. The information and the atmosphere crammed into those terse 140-character dispatches gripped the world's attention and galvanized resistance.

More than a year earlier, in December 2007, there was a similar reaction to the elections in Kenya, which led to weeks of violence and unrest throughout a country that many outsiders believed was one of the more stable democracies in Africa. At that time, with a media blackout in effect, one blogger became the focal point for reports and information from the ground. Tens of thousands of Kenyans and interested outsiders turned to this unofficial information resource to trade current, firsthand reports of riots, violence, troop movements, current rumors, and other critical information they desperately needed to see to their personal safety and that of their families.

This blogger, Ory Okolloh (AKA KenyanPundit), was a recent graduate of Harvard Law School who had returned home to Nairobi for what she thought would be a short break before beginning a career as a high-powered lawyer in Washington, D.C. During her schooling, she had taken an interest in technology as a tool of activism, and had started a blog with a few friends to keep track of the shenanigans of Kenya's members of parliament. By the time the election rolled around, she had already gained a reputation as an engaged critic and an uncompromising commentator, so it was natural that the politically and technologically aware segments of Kenya's growing young creative class would turn to her as a source of credible and authentic information.

"There was a government ban on live media and a wave of self-censorship within the mainstream media, which created an information vacuum" wrote Okolloh later. "The government argued that false and biased reporting would result in even more ethnic-based violence, and that it wanted the opportunity to review media reports before they went 'live.' In response to the ban, I asked people to send me information via comments on my blog and e-mails."[13]

After becoming overwhelmed and exhausted by the sheer volume of information, Okolloh thought it would be useful to have "a dedicated Web site where people could anonymously report incidents of violence online or by mobile phone text messages, and if this information could be mapped so that people could visualize what was going on."[14]

Shortly afterwards, she got together with Erik Hersman (whose blog, WhiteAfrican.com,[15] is a nexus in the burgeoning African ICT-entrepreneurial community), developer David Kobia, and activist Juliana Rotich, to form a company to develop and commercialize a platform that could serve as a hub for crowdsourced information during a crisis. They call their product and their company Ushahidi, which means "testimony" in Swahili.[16]

The company is organized as a 501(c)3 non-profit in the United States, but that is a mere formality. Ushahidi is a transnational cooperative in its management structure and its software development model: It depends extensively on the open source community for programming, testing, and new feature development. This organizational model not only fits the crowdsourced, bottom-up philosophy behind the product, but also turned out to be an extremely efficient and innovative way to mobilize global—and particularly African—IT talent around a compelling, socially useful project.

"We didn't deliberately have a strategy in place for the open source community," said Okolloh, who spoke to me in August 2009 from her current home in Johannesburg, South Africa. "When we did the original version of Ushahidi, there was no funding, no nothing. It was just a group of volunteers that got together, so in that sense, we

USHAHIDI CASE EXAMPLES

On its official Web site, the organization cites the following use-cases of its first-generation Ushahidi platform over the past several years:[17]

- *Stop Stockouts* is an initiative to track near real-time stockouts of medical supplies at pharmacies (in a medical store or health facility) in Kenya, Uganda, Malawi, and Zambia.
- *The Computer Professionals' Union* in the Philippines created the initiative called TXTpower, an effort to keep an eye on the mobile phone companies by ordinary citizens.
- *The Cuidemos el Voto mashup* is an independent platform to help monitor the federal elections of 5 July 2009 in Mexico.
- Ushahidi set up a site to track the *Swine Flu reports* coming in from official and unofficial sources at Swineflu.Ushahidi.com. The Team also created a way for citizen reports to be submitted (they remain unverified).
- *Vote Report India* is a collaborative citizen-driven election monitoring platform for the 2009 Indian general elections.
- *Al Jazeera* uses Ushahidi in their "War on Gaza" Web site covering the activity happening in Gaza in January 2009.
- *Unsung Peace Heroes* is a campaign developed by Butterfly Works and Media Focus on Africa Foundation. The goal is to nominate people who did extraordinary things for their fellow citizens or their country during and after the post-election violence in Kenya.
- *Kenya:* The initial mashup, used to track reports of incidents of violence around Kenya.
- *South Africa:* Used to map xenophobic attacks perpetrated against non-South Africans.

were always 'open source' from the beginning. The volunteer effort from the community coalesced around it and helped us produce the initial version of Ushahidi. It was a natural extension to reach out to the tech community at large, beyond the small group that had formed initially around it. We were aware that these people existed, but we did not anticipate getting the level of support that we did get. It was a challenge, because on one hand, we tried to push the project out as fast as we can, and on the other hand, we had to mix the paid staff and volunteers. Open source is not just a matter of putting a code out there—there's a whole protocol that goes along with it. That is something else we learned as we went along."

The disembodied, decentralized structure of the company is well-adapted to the environment in which it operates. "One of the beauties of technology is that it lowers the barriers to entry," said Okolloh. "We are able to approach it as a virtual organization thanks to Skype and phones and e-mail. We are able to get up and around pretty easily without having to look for office space, overhead, and things like that. Collaborate across borders, whatever. That definitely is something of an advantage, especially to the developing world."

At this early stage, Ushahidi relies primarily on grant funding, including a seed grant of $200,000 from Humanity United, which pays core staff and supports basic operating expenses. As is customary with open source projects, the Ushahidi product and the source code are distributed for free on the Web, but Okolloh says that the plan is to eventually move to a revenue model based on technical customization, installation, and support. Their marketing strategy to date has been viral, and the concept has already received a lot of attention in both the IT trade press and in development and crisis management circles.

In January, 2010, Ushahidi was put to one of its biggest and most public tests in the hours following the earthquake that devastated Haiti. The organization and its partners were among the first to start gathering real-time information for first-responders, aggregating incident reports on a real-time crisis map. This only enhanced the organization's prestige and visibility: Okolloh and Hersman now make the rounds at influential gatherings such as the World Economic Forum in Davos and the TED Conference, and publications like the "New York Times" and "Atlantic Monthly" are taking note.

Okolloh is very aware of the appeal of bringing cutting-edge technology to bear on an issue like crisis management, which draws a lot of attention from the global media. "It's something that has a lot of sexiness, global interest," she said. "Even though we are working on detailed issues, we have been able to get tremendous PR."

The attention is well-deserved. Ushahidi is at once a simple and revolutionary product. It is a technology platform or "engine" designed to allow anyone around the world to set up their own way to gather reports by mobile phone, e-mail, and the Web, and map them using Google Maps. Groups can customize the behavior and language of the interface for different locales and needs and use-case scenarios through plug-ins and extensions.

This creates a clearinghouse for information that planners can use to get an overview of crisis situations that is accurate with regard to time and place. It works by leveraging the rapid spread of personal communication technologies, including the Internet, but primarily mobile devices, SMS/text messaging, and camera phones. It is dependent on a critical mass of penetration of these devices and networks—a situation that did not exist even a few years ago.

With a strategic view of the situation, crisis response teams can make better decisions about where to deploy resources and put individual reports in the context of the overall situation as a way to help identify exaggerated or untrue information that might otherwise distort the response.

Okolloh says the growing success of Ushahidi is changing the way even large, well-established crisis response organizations like the Red Cross and United Nations Peacekeeping Forces manage information.

"I think they are definitely interested in different approaches," she explained. "Both have been receptive and have approached us independently." She said that internal bureaucracy is still a barrier to implementation. "It's not like, 'we're intrigued by this idea and we're going to implement it today.' [The decision-making] is a painful process. In real life, it takes dedicated resources to manage our product."

Despite these concerns, Okolloh is optimistic about the transformative potential. "There is interest, there is awareness within the organization that 'we don't know everything' and, with a top-down approach, you end up missing a lot of things. But I think the next step for bureaucracy is that you have to share that information, even with each other."

As with Steve Ressler's GovLoop, it may take the influence of an external platform to get the career professionals in large government and NGO agencies to emerge from their silos and start sharing information for common purpose. "We were talking with the UN Peacekeeping forces," said Okolloh. "They don't share information with each other, let alone with the outside. So it becomes somewhat contentious, especially about publicizing information. We've tried to convince them to at least start using it entirely with their own staffs. It's just going to take a lot more for them to make that transition from buying the idea to saying okay now, we're going to use this tool. But there's definitely a lot of interest, and there's definitely a lot of organizations that are trying to change their model."

Okolloh and her team fit many of the characteristics of the Young World entrepreneur. Once part of the African diaspora, Okolloh decided to return to her homeland ("because I was more needed there"). Because of her blogging activities, she found herself at the center of important events and took that opportunity to build an organization that blends public and private, social and commercial aspects to solve a problem that is felt most acutely in less well-resourced societies. Both Ushahidi's approach and its development model are steeped in wikinomic, crowdsourced ideology, which turn out to be both effective and sustainable in the context in which it is operating. The organization is proudly virtual, and depends on the discretionary effort of a worldwide community for its very existence.

Okolloh said that providing opportunities for recognition and income for volunteers is a big part of Ushahidi's strategy. "It's something that we do very deliberately. I always emphasize this when I talk about Ushahidi: Our team is a team of volunteer developers— primarily African. This is very much an African initiative, and this is what we're capable of. If you dig down, you might find more talent in development. There's a lot of stuff going on. But also think of [the effect on the] African [workforce], to think that there are opportunities out there that if you brush up your skills, work as a professional."

Its product builds bridges to connect public, private, and NGO resources to help address a critical need that is acutely felt in the developing world. And Okolloh and Hersman are aware of the value of their example and the importance of blazing trails that others can follow.

"I definitely think we are part of a larger movement," said Okolloh. "Primarily because of technology and the space that we're working in, it's hot and it's interesting. I cannot overemphasize this: The technology makes it easy to put out our facts on that map, for people to take notice of us, while at the same time addressing our deeper, more serious issues."

REACHING THE GLOBAL MARKET WITH INNOVATIVE PRODUCTS AND SERVICES

Unleashing Invention in the Young World: DUTO (Colombia)

When inventors invent and creators create, the ingenuity and audacity of their innovations can be astonishing. This is true of innovation throughout history, not just in the tech-centric present day. Equally true is that great ideas can come from anywhere. You don't have to be well educated and certainly not well-connected to experience that moment of inspiration in which a long-sought solution or great new vision presents itself. However, until recently, access to the resources necessary to move from that "aha!" moment of ideation and breakthrough and down the long road to market was restricted to those in proximity to centers of capital and business knowledge. Now, global information networks are opening the floodgates for innovators everywhere to compete for resources and markets on the basis of their merits.

The Young World entrepreneurs unleashed into the wider world are often focused most intently on the gaps that they perceive in their own surroundings. This can lead to the development of new products that focus on needs ignored by larger companies. Few examples illustrate this point better than DUTO, S.A., a startup company from the remote mountains of Colombia. DUTO devised an innovative touch-screen display to enable visually-impaired students to experience online educational materials through their hands, interpreting the shapes and colors of images into sensations on a touch pad. DUTO's product, IRIS, is now in advanced prototype, and the company hopes to begin regional distribution in Colombia and neighboring countries by 2012.

DUTO is a commercial venture with a strong social dimension. However, the company is not only an example of Young World entrepreneurship that combines social purpose and market-minded ingenuity; it is also a case study of how great ideas that emerge far from the established centers of innovation and finance can find their way into the mainstream using resources and networks that simply did not exist just a decade ago.

DUTO rose from modest beginnings. In 2003, María Fernanda Zúñiga Zabala, John Alexis Guerra Gómez, and Filipe Restrepo Calle were undergraduates at the Universidad Tecnológica de Pereida, high in the mountainous coffee-growing region of Colombia. They needed to come up with a team project for their senior thesis in computer science and they hit on the idea of creating a solution for people with visual disabilities. This was an ambitious concept, particularly since their university was not regarded as a major research center.

"Everybody told us we were crazy, that we would not be able to finish this as an undergrad thesis," said Guerra, now working on his Ph.D. as a Fulbright Scholar at the University of Maryland. "But actually we finished it and after that came a process in which we created a company."

After graduation, they continued to develop their product, recruiting two other members to their team. They entered the 2007 TIC Americas competition and sprinted away with the top prize.

"DUTO is amazing for many reasons, not only for the product, but also because of the where it came from," said Young Americas Business Trust Executive Director Luis Viguria. "They are from a very small town. They are really poor guys, you can't imagine. Before TIC Americas [provided them with recognition], people would say, 'no, you are from the back country, you are not supposed to create [information] technologies. You are supposed to start a family and grow coffee.' But instead, they chose to create something that will make a difference, perhaps for thousands or millions of people. That is how you can change people's mentality with just a program."

DUTO took the money they won and created a new prototype. They took it to Asia and competed in the global TIC, won there, reinvested that money in a refined prototype, and took it all around the world to showcase for potential investors, partners, distributors, and customers. By 2008, they had secured a contract to deploy a pilot test in Pereida, but the financial crisis put those plans on hold.

"We have already spent and invested more than $250,000 doing all of this research, creating a lot of patents, and the prototypes," said Guerra. "It's a long process, but we need to take this product to market. We're waiting for the last push to get us to that point."

Guerra said he and his partners took the path of entrepreneurship partly to make a difference and partly out of necessity. "The reason why we have all these entrepreneurs in Colombia is that if you don't create your own company, it's very possible you won't get a job, because there are not enough jobs. That is one of the reasons why you have so many startups there. The other reason is that Colombia is making a bid for entrepreneurism, so they are offering a lot of funds like angel capital and a lot of money that you don't have to give back when you do what you say you are doing. So when we say we are creating this device for blind people and it's something really crazy because nobody has done it in the world, they believe in you and they give you money like they did with us."

Another important factor is the social acceptance of entrepreneurism within the Colombian culture. "We have in our blood to be entrepreneurs," said Guerra. "In Colombia we have this tradition; we are business people and we love to do business and create organizations. So when the entrepreneur [trend] came, it was something familiar to us. On top of that, you have something you really need to create entrepreneurs, that is, to encourage companies to develop themselves, you have the support that the government is giving us, and the universities and educational organizations that are giving a lot of information in how to create business plans and how to create companies. So it's a really nice mixture that helps to create this."

Beyond the support provided by the government of Colombia, Guerra also points to the importance of global networks—both formal and informal—that have transformed the climate for entrepreneurs in the Young World over the past decade. "At this moment we have the networks and the knowledge to find where the opportunities are," he said with enthusiasm. "When you are just starting as an entrepreneur, you are completely unknown. The biggest challenge is how to connect these young, really smart people in whatever they are doing. It doesn't matter if they are a social entrepreneur or just an entrepreneur looking for money. Whatever the situation is, the question is how to connect them with the correct resources. It is really amazing just to see how many people are speaking about social entrepreneurism and how to donate things, how much money [is] available for everybody. But then you go back to my country, and you have all these really smart guys, really smart girls who have really interesting ideas, but you cannot connect them. But something I can tell you is that I believe: because of DUTO, there have been new opportunities that have been open for other organizations in our city and in our country."

Organizing Local Industries for Global Customers: Thrillophilia (India) and StarSoft (India)

For knowledge-economy entrepreneurship to really make a difference in Young World economies, it needs to spread beyond the narrow base of the software and technology industries. Many Young World markets are characterized by large numbers of small, family-owned businesses or independent providers who lack the competencies and the resources to be visible and competitive beyond their local customer base. As technology and globalization bring the world crashing in to their small, unorganized markets, they need to embrace greater transparency and standard business practices to compete. It is increasingly falling to indigenous ICT entrepreneurs to help small businesses in more traditional sectors of the economy adapt, and thus survive, amid rapid change.

One important way that knowledge-industry entrepreneurs can help traditional small businesses adapt to a global economy is to provide the superstructure of organization to the market as a whole that the businesses themselves, as small entities, cannot.

Consider the example of the tourism industry. Tourism is not a matter of life or death like AIDS prevention or disaster relief, but it is a huge source of foreign exchange to countries where high-value exports are in short supply. Especially in middle- or lower-income countries, such as Mexico, India, Thailand and Egypt, much of that business is done by local providers: hotels, guest houses, tour operators, souvenir vendors, and so on, who engage foreign visitors in one-off transactions. In poorer Young World countries—and in many rich, old ones as well—this situation creates temptations for unscrupulous operators to take advantage of tourists, who have little practical recourse if the costs or the experience do not match their expectations. In an environment where it is difficult to judge from afar who is honest and who is not, ethical actors are not guaranteed an economic reward for their honesty, while shoddy businesses can prosper without penalty. Anyone who has visited a popular tourist spot in a developing country knows what I am talking about. Government regulations work only insofar as inspections are current and regulators are honest, neither of which can be guaranteed, and many of the providers are too small to be governed by industry or government standards in any case.

This is more likely to be a problem in niche areas of travel and tourism such as eco-tourism or adventure travel, where norms are still evolving and the clientele is considered less desirable by government tourism ministries than the five-star cruise-ship set. India, for example, is expanding its tourist repertoire beyond the tried-and-true itinerary of ancient temples and historical sites to include adventure travel activities, such as trekking, cross-country bicycling, scuba diving, and the various "extreme" outdoor sports favored by the Millennial generation. It's a huge revenue opportunity. However, the network of local firms that caters to this particular adventure niche is especially informal. Some are excellent. Others economize in ways that you would not want to discover when you are scuba-diving 50 meters below the ocean's surface or paragliding 100 meters above it. Few of the firms have recognized "brands," and even online user ratings might not tell the full story.

This is not just an issue for foreign tourists. India's expanding young middle class finds itself equally frustrated by the lack of consistent standards and good information. The problem is that if enough people have bad experiences, it diminishes the reputation of the entire region, which hurts everyone's business. This is frustrating to the good operators, who can only run their businesses according to their own standards and have no control over the actions of their competitors. They don't have the resources or the credibility to differentiate themselves in the emerging global marketplace: They just have to take their chances with everyone else and hope their high standards eventually translate to better results.

In 2007, five young adventure travel aficionados from Bangalore, India's high-tech hub, decided to apply the skills they learned (and the money they made) working for top-level multinational technology companies, to bring some order to this disorganized market. They founded a company, Thrillophilia,[18] that provides reliable information about the best adventure travel destinations and local businesses available to a Web-savvy global clientele by employing state-of-the-art social media technology and design aesthetics. In typical Young World style, their enterprise combines personal interest with systemic benefit, and profit with public good.

I met with two of the five founding partners, Abhishek Daga and Chitra Gurnani, at a quiet restaurant in Bangalore's Vashant Nagar district. An attractive, earnest young couple, Abhishek and Chitra exude passion for their work. Not only did they seem relieved to be out of the software and services rat race (Chitra worked at Infosys, Abhishek for Cisco), they have that rare glow of people who love what they are doing.

"We could no longer work for other people. We had to work for ourselves," explained Abhishek. "All five of us [founding partners] love adventure travel and we saw a great opportunity to combine our passion with good business."

It was a hard road at first. They launched their company with their own savings and the support of their families. The partners, who all work in the high-tech industry, are leaving their jobs in phases to keep the cash flowing (Abhishek was still transitioning out of his role at Cisco when we met), but the whole idea of moving from the certainty of gainful employment to the risk of entrepreneurship is a new development among the current generation of young Indians. Indeed, some older friends and relatives wondered aloud if they had lost their minds, leaving such desirable jobs to chase a dream. After several years, they are starting to see some momentum build behind their efforts, and have lately been rebuffing the advances of venture capitalists.

To entrepreneurs in developed countries, there is nothing interesting or unusual here: Business creation carries risk, including the risk of lost opportunities. Those are the rules of the game. In Young World countries, however, the road to the top is still narrow and the distance to the bottom is quite far. Most people in those societies do not feel comfortable risking the kind of failure that is a necessary ingredient of innovation, absent a long cultural or family tradition of entrepreneurship, or profound economic necessity. The willingness of people like Abhishek and his partners to take meaningful risks not just to create economic opportunities for themselves—they had good jobs, after all—but simply to pursue their passion, represents an important maturation of the entrepreneurial climate at the top edge of the Young World, and is a trend worth watching.

Abhishek and Chitra walked me through the early days of Thrillophilia. The group began collecting experiences and sharing them on a Web site, building an adventure travel "bible" that now spans more than 350 pages. They fanned out across the country, inspecting various local companies, interviewing managers and staff, checking equipment, comparing prices, and swapping stories with other hardcore thrill seekers.

"Safety and quality are our top concerns," said Chitra. "With this kind of travel, you don't want people cutting corners to try to make more money for themselves." Many small vendors don't measure up to the company's standards. "They don't think long-term about their brand or reputation. It's all about how can I take maximum advantage right now."

Chitra said those kinds of experiences turn tourists sour on the whole industry and make it difficult for the good firms to succeed. Part of Thrillophilia's mission is to create more visibility and a blanket global brand for the top local companies, drive more business to them, and realign the incentives of the industry to focus more on the long term. Local providers who meet Thrillophilia's high standards are rewarded with long-term booking agreements, and benefit from the company's state-of-the-art marketing capabilities.

Abhishek manages the Thrillophilia Web site, which he keeps constantly up to date with fresh content and the latest technology. "Several hours a day, I try to educate myself about new social media platforms, new methods of search engine optimization, and new ways to reach customers without spamming them." He combs various social sites including Digg, Okrut, Twitter, and Facebook to find conversations about people travelling to India, and approaches them in a respectful, low-key way that resonates with his Net Generation peers around the world. "We are looking for ways to integrate video and geolocation services into the site in the next year or two," he said. "The more vivid an experience we can provide, the more interest we can generate."

Companies like Thrillophilia not only create commercial opportunities for themselves and their partners, they are also helping an entire segment of the tourism industry raise its performance to global standards by providing incentives and opportunities for the formation of social capital that did not exist before. Their bottom–up approach supports vibrant and diverse local competition, as opposed to a top-down regulatory scheme that fosters uniformity and stifles innovation. Because Abhishek and his friends decided to take a risk to follow their passion, an entire ecosystem of small businesses gains a point of entry into the global market and an important incentive to improve their own performance.

* * *

Down the road from Bangalore in the city of Mysore, another small entrepreneur is bringing modern tech savvy to an ancient industry. Textile production is so quintessentially Indian that a spinner's wheel is featured on the national flag. Mahatma Gandhi used to spin yarn to clear his mind, and celebrated the homely craft in his writings. These days, globalization and mass manufacturing have put local textile production under increasing pressure. Even family firms that modernized earlier in the century find their traditional way of life thrown into uncertainty by vast, impersonal economic forces.

The traditional techniques of spinning are highly specialized and not easily amenable to automation. The market itself is comprised of many small businesses and cottage industries that individually lack buying power, not to mention the education or cultural orientation to embrace information technology. It is not an attractive market for software vendors, and consequently there has not been much investment in creating products to help these businesses lift their productivity and practices to the standards demanded by an increasingly competitive global economy.

Kalpesh Mehta came from a family in Mysore that supported textile spinners throughout India, but he resisted going into the family business. After completing his education in engineering in the late 1990s, he decided to apply his IT skills to create software built specifically to the needs of the local spinners, presented in a way that was simple and intuitive enough for small business people to grasp without extensive training.

"I spent eight months to a year just observing the process in great detail," said Mehta, an intense, soft-spoken young man, when we spoke poolside at a hotel in downtown Mysore. "I wanted to be sure that what I created did not require the spinners to depart from their usual practices. The goal was to give the business owner a better idea of the resources being used at each stage of the process. They need that kind of visibility to improve their performance and remain profitable."

Mehta says that a new generation was taking over family businesses at that time, and some of the new young owners were more interested in IT solutions than their more traditional parents. What began as a project for his own family business became a commercial product and the basis for Mehta's own firm StarSoft, which he launched in 2001.

"In the course of developing the textile software, I discovered I had a talent for breaking down complex processes into steps that could be put into an application framework," he said. He started building a small team of developers in an office space adjacent to the family textile business and earned a Microsoft Gold partner certification to help obtain clients for broader software development services.

"Our next project was to build a transaction engine for micro-credit," said Shailendra Rao Nalige, strategic advisor to StarSoft. "Extending banking services to rural and low-income populations is a big priority for both the government and the private sector in India right now, but it requires a specialized platform that can handle small transactions and caters to people with very little banking or computer experience."

Mehta's attention to detail and understanding of the target audience helped StarSoft develop a competitive product. They are now working on a new version that takes advantage of a services-based architecture to make the processes available securely over the Web. In the meantime, StarSoft keeps the revenues flowing by providing outsourced technical services to businesses in the United States, Europe, and the Middle East.

What began as a commercial venture to serve one of the most traditional sectors of the economy has nevertheless evolved into a company culture that fits the pattern of many of the successful Young World knowledge-services businesses that I interviewed worldwide. "The atmosphere of the company is very open and very inspiring," said Vaseem Mohammed, StarSoft's 28-year-old account manager, who was recruited to join the company from a previous position in customer support. "Rather than sticking to routine and structure, everyone is encouraged to contribute."

StarSoft's story is not unusual in the booming software and services economy of India, but it is notable that this particular business got its start—and still has roots—in a mission to use technology to empower and organize an ancient industry, rather than simply try to cash in on the global ousourcing boom.

ACHIEVING ESCAPE VELOCITY

Most of the organizations discussed up until this point fit the category of small businesses, and it is reasonable to wonder whether the unique Young World traits I have imputed to them, particularly their agility, culture, opportunistic use of networks and technologies, and ability to find and fill market gaps, are simply the attributes of any new startup in the current climate. If that were the case, their emergence would constitute an interesting but not terribly disruptive development in the long term, because one might assume that as the businesses grow beyond their founders' initial visions, they will begin adopting the characteristics of traditional managerial companies anywhere.

One way to test that theory is to look at a few examples of Young World enterprises that have grown into successful global providers of the very first rank. Ghana's theSOFTtribe, Argentina's Globant, and India's Infosys all epitomize Young World knowledge economy entrepreneurism at its most mature stage: strategic, multinational, well-resourced, and highly competitive for both business and talent.

In each case, we see that the Young World differentiators have not diminished with the increase in scale; rather, they have become even more pronounced. These companies all invest massively in local capacity development; seek alignment between public, private, and NGO resources for both business and social purposes; capitalize on distributed workforce and networked business models; and focus on an ethos of sustainability firmly rooted in the Spartan conditions of their home markets.

Most importantly, each of these companies fulfills a critical role in their national and regional entrepreneurial ecosystems. They are beacons of success, changing the way young people think about their potential. They create wealth and employment, giving rise to a whole ancillary system of suppliers within and beyond the knowledge economy sector, with implications that ripple across the social, political, and economic spectra. They influence education and infrastructure policy, and furnish knowledge and material support to institutions that cultivate new business development and entrepreneurship. These effects are not mere byproducts of their commercial success, but deliberate strategies organic to their missions, motivated by market considerations combined with national pride and purpose.

The various organizations described up until this point are relay stations in the emerging network of Young World entrepreneurship. Companies like the three described next are the dynamos, generating the energy that is rapidly creating a much more complex, multi-polar world of business.

Knocking Down Barriers: theSOFTtribe (Ghana)

"Is there an African Infosys or Microsoft on the horizon somewhere?" I asked Erik Hersman, an expert on the African IT scene and co-founder of Ushahidi, toward the conclusion of our interview.

"Well, you know, the closest to that may well be theSOFTtribe in Ghana, started by Herman Chinery-Hesse," said Hersman without much of a pause. "They make business software specific for the African market. He's probably been the most successful with it, and it's been really interesting to watch him over the past 10–15 years."

If anything, Hersman may have been conservative in his judgment. *Inc.* Magazine ran a profile of Chinery-Hesse in its October 2008 issue under the headline "Meet the Bill Gates of Africa."[19]

The comparison is apt, not only because the two men share a passion for creating software, but also because their vision transcends business and foresees massive transformations in the lives of billions. At a time when Africa's economic and political misfortunes dominated perceptions of the continent, Chinery-Hesse saw a bright future in the unique opportunities posed by knowledge-economy entrepreneurship. "Technology is the only way for Africa to get rich," he was quoted in an interview with the BBC. "We don't have proper infrastructure and we can't compete in manufacturing. But if you put me behind a PC and tell me to write software for a Chinese customer, then I can compete brain for brain with anyone trying to do the same thing in the U.S."[20]

Chinery-Hesse grew up as the son of educated elites in West Africa (his mother still serves as an advisor to Ghana's president), went to high school in Austin, Texas, and studied industrial technology at Texas State University in San Marcos. After spending a short time in the United Kingdom trying to establish himself, Chinery-Hesse made the fateful decision to return to Ghana in 1991 to start a business in an industry that few people in the region considered viable: software development.

"When I first started the business, people thought it was a joke," reminisced Chinery-Hesse from his home in Accra, when we spoke in early August of 2009. "Everybody thought technology was something that was imported, especially high-tech, like software."

But the young entrepreneur, who had learned his business skills working as a garage mechanic in Freetown, Sierra Leone, as a teenager, was determined to prove the critics wrong. Chinery-Hesse recognized that commercial software products developed in and for the mature markets of North America, Europe and East Asia assumed the presence of certain conditions that did not apply in places like West Africa—conditions such as a reliable communications and power grid, the presence of trained and honest workers, and businesses that could afford to pay high prices for information services.

Chinery-Hesse and his partner, Joe Jackson, launched theSOFT-tribe[21] in 1991 to meet the real world needs of businesses operating in more rugged terrains. theSOFTtribe developed the concept of *tropical tolerance*: "Basically, that's where the tech is immune to some degree to four things: communication challenges, power challenges, people challenges, and cost challenges," explained Chinery-Hesse. "These were the guidelines that we used to fashion our software."

During the 1990s, theSOFTtribe grew by leaps and bounds, becoming the dominant software for business management, accounting, payroll and financial reporting throughout English-speaking West Africa. Then, suddenly, the growth slowed almost to a halt. The problem was that theSOFTtribe sold primarily to commercial businesses, but in their markets, the private sector only accounted for 40% of the economy. Government spending, driven by huge infusions of foreign aid, represented the most significant share of the IT spend. Penetrating that market provided Chinery-Hesse and his team with a frustrating lesson in the realities of globalization.

"We realized that we had outgrown the private sector and [needed] some big government contracts," said Chinery-Hesse. "The foreign governments and banks that were loaning our governments money to buy technology were opposed to them buying local. They would say, 'if we're giving you a grant and you're going to spend that on software, then you better buy an international brand name because we don't want you to waste the money . . . and it's our money!'"

The politics surrounding the awarding of aid-driven contracts sparks Chinery-Hesse's passion. "In our own market, we, the local company, are the one getting thrown off the table, due to this colonial-style interference from the international organizations," he said. "They favor their nationals in the procurement, so they throw all kinds of technicalities in. They do not exactly tell our governments 'go buy American, go buy British, go buy European.' They can't tell them that. All they tell them is the companies bidding must have turned over five million dollars in the last two years; the company must be an international company. In one case, I argued that we are international. We have products in Ghana, Nigeria, Bukino Faso, Togo, and Gambia. Why aren't you accepting that we are international? They said, 'we didn't mean *that*.' They mean 'Western.'"

Chinery-Hesse realized that he needed an international partner as the price of admission to the lavish banquet of government contracts being catered by Western banks and aid dollars. The company did an analysis of suitable products in the market and found a match in Navision, a business management software originally developed in Scandinavia but recently acquired by Microsoft as part of its Microsoft Dynamics portfolio. "Microsoft Navision is a software development platform which is well-suited for our environment. And we benefited from the Microsoft name, and the branding, and the market language, so we were able to shut up the community in their quest to not have local companies get the contracts. We said we were also Microsoft, and that kind of worked."

By marrying its own deep expertise in the local market with the advantages afforded by the Microsoft brand and Navision technology, theSOFTtribe made immediate inroads into the public sector. "Oracle did the government payroll of Ghana for like 10 years, with all kinds of problems," said Chinery-Hesse. "They were not able to fix it. Back and forth, back and forth. Being called Microsoft, we went for a tender two years ago and we won. And we took it away. In fact, they stopped the Oracle system that was running and started up our system, our own payroll system which we migrated onto the Microsoft platform. In eight weeks, we managed to achieve what Oracle could not achieve in ten years. It was cheaper and more efficient. We needed the Microsoft name to be able to do it. We had to take our existing products, which essentially dominated the private sector anyway, convert them onto a Microsoft back end so we could call it Microsoft, then we took that product into the tender and we cleaned everybody out. We were allowed to eat at the table because our products were called Microsoft."

Chinery-Hesse has had greater success in recent years winning contracts from African governments, but he is adamant that the African IT industry cannot progress until the buying power of the private sector increases. His latest venture, Africa Business Source,[22] is an ambitious effort to jumpstart that kind of economic development by giving African small and medium enterprises (SMEs) the same kind of direct access to global markets as sellers have on Western trading platforms like eBay and Amazon's zStores.

Despite the late hour of our conversation, Chinery-Hesse grew increasingly animated describing the vision for his new project. "The majority of Africans don't live in the big cities. They live in the bush. Those people have never been connected to global trade. Never. If you are sitting in the African bush and you have two African drums, and there was somebody in California who wanted to buy them, there is no way for you to know, no way for them to pay you, no way you can advertise your wares. You don't understand international exports in the bush where you are. There's no Web developer either. These people form the majority in Africa. Now what I'm doing is using technology to connect them to the global marketplace, by setting up an African eBay, and African PayPal, so you can live in the bush, have your mobile phone, make African drums, sell them at $500 a pop, and suddenly sell 10 drums a week. And, like Americans, become millionaires. We can take local mom and pop shops and evolve them into global providers. That opportunity has never existed."

Chinery-Hesse sees tens of thousands of local businesses, in areas ranging from books and music to curios to travel and tourism services to high-end software development services, benefiting from a platform that gives them direct access to high-end customers beyond their borders. "They'll expand with our economy. I expect all of those merchants will start making money. They are not government, and they are not influenced [by the politics of foreign aid], and they will buy my software. So I run two companies. And I expect the latter to be a catalyst for the former in the medium term. There are all those people in the bush, making drums and masks and so on for export, who [could] become multimillion dollar companies. They will need software. And they will behave rationally, and they will buy local. Not because of tribalism or nationalism. They will buy local because it is cheaper and better and better supported. With no influence."

With a systematic approach to entrepreneurism resonant of Peter Drucker, Chinery-Hesse has identified the structural barriers in his business environment and is inventing his way around them. It turns out that those barriers happen to be the more formidable problems of governance, aid, dependency, and neo-colonialism that have hamstrung African economic development since independence. Regardless, he is undaunted.

"I've come to accept that for now, the public sector is going to be a liability. Their incentive structures are such that it is more important for them to be on good terms with the World Bank than with the local business community. That's just the way it is. So the indigenous business community needs to expand to where it can run independent of the politicians, to where the politicians will now need to come and court the local business community.

"Even if this halfway works, even if we do half of what we intend to achieve, the impact will be massive and will align everybody's interest. If a government continues to pass these anti-African, pro-Western laws, the democracy will work and they will be thrown out of office before you can say jack. Because it will be tangible and real. Right now, there are so many people . . . what, three-fifths of the economy, the people, are outside the major economy? They are in the informal economy. They are hanging around doing subsistence farming. So if the government passes a law that says that everybody shall now be taxed at 50%, it doesn't affect them. They don't pay tax. If they pay tax, they can't see it. Tax is in the kerosene they bought for their lantern. They just know prices have gone up. They don't realize government jacked up taxes. So after a while, they . . . everybody . . . are being hit with a ridiculous income tax and harassment from civil servants and so on.

"As a group, they will take these people down. And that's what I'm hoping for."

Taking on the World: Globant (Argentina)

In 2002, Argentina was in the midst of a financial crisis. The government had just decided to devalue the currency in hopes of reducing the burden of the country's external debt and making its exports more competitive on the world market.

Martín Migoya, Martín Umaran, Guibert Englebienne and Néstor Nocetti, four young rising stars in the IT and software development industry who had been working abroad for large, multinational companies, met in a bar in downtown Buenos Aires. For some time, they had perceived a gap in the regional software market. Local developers sold to local companies, larger firms turned to multinationals or providers from places like India, Ireland, and Israel, but there was no clear leader in all of Latin America with the resources and ambition to compete in the global market for IT services and software.

Given the depth of the local talent pool, the proximity and time-zone compatibility with customers in North America and Europe, the physical and social amenities of Buenos Aires as a tool for attracting new talent and customers, and the ability to tap into global markets from anywhere via networks, there was already plenty of potential. All that was needed was a catalyst.

The four men quit their well-paid jobs and set out to prove that Argentina—and indeed other parts of South and Central America—could be an IT outsourcing center to rival India and the other emerging leaders. They envisioned a firm that could operate at the highest international standards and serve as the hub of a new ecosystem of technology-based businesses to serve international customers. They opened their doors in 2003 and called their new company Globant.[23]

The devaluation crisis opened a window of opportunity in which Argentine firms could compete at a cost advantage and cement relationships that could see them through the early stages of growth. Despite great initial difficulties getting financing, Globant was able to secure enough business to steadily increase in size and capabilities. Though they started out following the simple IT services outsourcing model of Indian companies, they soon discovered opportunities to move higher up the value chain, as a full partner in design and innovation.

"We were four in 2003, now we are 1,400 and growing at a fast pace," said Guibert Englebeinne, Globant's CTO, as he relaxed in the conference room of the company's Buenos Aires headquarters on a cool September afternoon. "Our exports account for 95% of our revenues, and 60% of our revenues are coming from Silicon Valley, from companies that are innovative, that value the kind of service that we provide." He proudly ticked off a client list that includes a who's who of Internet and entertainment industries: Yahoo, LinkedIn, Friendster, Electronic Arts, Nike, Disney, Dreamworks. In 2006, Google selected Globant as the first company which they trusted to do some of their development outside of Googleplex. Google's Latin American director, Gonzalo Alonso, became so enamored with his new partner that he left his job to join Globant in April 2009.

When asked by the online publication VentureBeat whether he considered leaving Google a risk, Alonso replied "Not chasing my dream to be part of a Latin American multinational that competes globally was the only risk."[24]

So what kind of company can lure a rising executive away from Google? Globant is not only focused on innovation (and, of course, profit)—it also prides itself on a corporate culture that sounds more reminiscent of a San Francisco dotcom from the 1990s than a typical Argentine business.

"Our aim was twofold," explained Englebienne. "One was to try to create a company with a value proposition that was differentiated to the customers. I believe we are doing that. We are obtaining a lot of recognition. We are an MIT business case, we have been selected as one of the top ten application development houses in the world, entrepreneur of the year . . . many awards. But on the other side, we are creating a culture that fosters innovation and is totally unique in our environment, and leading to the creation of an industry that I believe has a lot to offer to our people."

To summarize the core values of the company, the partners issued a manifesto on Globant's fifth anniversary. Top items: Act ethically and think big. Last item: Have fun. "From the manifesto you can extrapolate first of all a patriotic sentimental emphasis on the importance of creating a big multinational from a place that is mostly known for beef and nice-looking ladies," said Englebienne with a disarming smile. "Having a firm that creates opportunities; that is extremely important. Also, we are trying to inspire a group to [feel part of] a world-class business environment. That, unfortunately, is not always the case in Argentina. And also one important thing, have fun. You know? Have fun with your work, have fun with the people you work with."

Globant's culture, which echoes the atmosphere fostered by Suhas Gopinath halfway around the world at the similarly named and similarly oriented Globals, Inc., acts like a magnet for Net Generation talent and an incubator for the kind of creative skills and out-of-the-box thinking that the company needs to serve its demanding clientele. "Our passion is to avoid having our people emigrate," said Englebienne. "We would like to say that we import opportunities and we export software."

Because the founders of Globant are interested in creating a regional industry and not just a standalone company, they invest heavily in capacity building and spreading the gospel of entrepreneurship throughout Argentina.

"We are thinking long-term and about scale," said Englebienne. "One thing that we've been working on this year, together with a group at MIT, is Globant University, a program to connect the requirements of our customers in the high-tech sector with the vocational systems here and the education system. We need to be able to increase the dynamics of producing talent and create a streamlined supply chain for talent."

Englebienne sees the growth of indigenous entrepreneurship and the move toward bottom-up, community-based organizations as the vehicle that will propel countries like Argentina into the first ranks of the global economy. "The most important impact we could have would not be what Globant is able to achieve *per se*, but in the very large number of companies that will be created by people exposed to what we do, either by being employees or people that we connect to."

Englebienne is especially proud of Globant's active in promoting entrepreneurship in Argentina. "I'm trying to expose our case as much as we can," he said. "There is not a single day in which we don't need to do a presentation in the university or in an entrepreneurial meeting or whatever. We base a lot of potential on inspiring other entrepreneurs to do the same thing that we do and try to share good practices among us. I believe of course there are a number of companies who have been able to, who are starting up all day, and thinking global, and not only focused on IT, but on other provisioning services such as health care, architecture, and other areas."

Globant's partners believe that creating a new environment from the bottom up is what is required to change the shape of communities in Latin America. "I wouldn't expect a lot coming from the top, coming from our elites, the political class. I think there is a lot to be gained from entrepreneurs bottom up, and creating and inspiring others to create companies and create value. So this is something that inspires us to continue to win."

Leading and Seeding Innovation: Infosys (India)

Finally we come to the prototype and pinnacle of Young World entrepreneurism, Infosys. Because the Indian IT services giant has been so transformative and so disruptive of the global economy, so celebrated (most notably by Thomas Friedman), and so wildly commercially successful, it is possible to forget that the company rose from rather humble and unlikely origins, as the brainchild of seven software developers in Bangalore in the early 1980s.

Infosys itself certainly has not forgotten. As the centerpiece of India's knowledge economy and the hub of a massive ecosystem that it conjured into being either directly or indirectly, Infosys is intensely aware how the economic future of literally billions of people rests on its actions and its investments. At the same time, it is a player at the highest levels of the lucrative IT services marketplace, competing with the likes of IBM and Accenture for multimillion dollar corporate and government contracts around the world.

Because of this dual role, Infosys embodies and constantly redefines the endpoint of all the aspects of Young World entrepreneurship discussed throughout this chapter, even though it long ago moved into a more mature phase of corporate existence.

Infosys made its reputation and its billions through outsourcing, a term the company practically invented. The value proposition is to provide critical business services better and at lower costs than companies can do for themselves. In earlier days, Infosys was able to compete strictly on the basis of the lower costs of the Indian labor market.

Those days are mostly done. World-class talent attracts world-class salaries, and for less demanding kinds of work, Infosys's competitors have established their own operations in India and elsewhere, tapping into the same general labor markets and cost structures. The company knows that its leadership position in the future depends on maintaining its advantage in talent, performance, and innovation, not just cost.

Fortunately, Infosys sits on top of the world's most abundant supply of human capital. India's education system churns out more than 200,000 engineers per year, 10 times the number produced in the United States, and slightly ahead of China.* Infosys rides it reputation as India's most desirable employer to garner a mind-boggling 1 million employment applications per year for an average of 25,000 new positions.

Nandita Gurjar, Infosys Senior VP for Global Human Resources, says that the company could fill its ranks only from the topmost tier of universities nationwide, but broadens the search to more than 1,000 institutions as part of a deliberate strategy. "Frankly, we could only hire from the top 250 colleges and we would have managed to get our best," she said, when we met at the Infosys campus in Bangalore. "It's aspirational for us to go to those [second-tier] colleges and hire at least 10 students, or 5 students sometimes, so that they go back and say 'this is what you can become.' In every part of our process, we have what we call a *sustainability question*, which asks 'How are you building a sustainable organization?' And for me a very large part is to say that I am building a society which can continue to produce these people. Because if we lose the advantage of continuously having a large number of bright people coming up, then the whole India story is over."

The problem is that many of the recruits lack that polish of employability that we've seen come up so often in discussions of Young World workforce development. Independent organizations such as NASSCOM and voices in the Indian media routinely decry the lack of fitness of most university graduates and exhort policy-makers to reform or reinvent the educational system.

---

* Note that China's definition of engineering is rather broad, and even the country's most accomplished students must also master English in addition to their technical subject matter to be employable at the global level.

Like many of the smaller, less-established Young World companies profiled earlier, Infosys does not wait for institutional solutions to appear from the top down, but takes an active role in aligning resources, and, to a great extent, filling the workforce capacity gaps through its own investments. And as with many things in India, those investments operate at a scale almost inconceivable to outsiders.

Infosys has focused on training and mentorship since its earliest days (co-founder and Chairman Narayana Murthy still retains the title "Chief Mentor"). As its fortunes in the global economy have improved, it has plowed more and more resources into education to close the gaps between the still-evolving Indian higher education system and the demands of the global knowledge marketplace. The showpiece of the company's efforts is a sprawling residential training facility in Mysore.

"That facility has about 1.5 million square feet of education space, where we can train about 13,500 people on a single day. 10,000 people can reside in the campus," said Tan Moorthy, VP of Research and Education. "Our intent is to help the fresh students who make the transition into the corporate world. This is done through interventions which have the component of soft skills, training, understanding corporate etiquette, understanding communications skills, all of those, and then getting into the sense of computing and computer systems, operating systems, programming languages, databases, and so forth."

The importance of Infosys's investment in human capital is not lost on India's policy-makers. On the day we met, Moorthy was in Mysore to commemorate the opening of a new extension to the campus with Sonia Gandhi, India's leading political figure.

So why go to the lengths of having a 29-week residential program for new employees? "We understand that there is a lot of *unlearning* that our Indian students need to do before they start becoming global," said Gurjar. "It requires a residential immersion program whereby they are taught to do different things which make them more global citizens than just Indian. Most of them have never been out of the country, they've not flown on an aircraft, they've not spoken to people with different cultures, and we need them to get fast-tracked on that very quickly. So while the four months seems as though it's largely on a technical program, getting them up to speed, there's a large part of our values, our code of conduct—this is the way we work, this the way do things out here—which is a very strong immersion program we have there."

One of the biggest hurdles is convincing the products of one of the world's most competitive, test-driven educational systems to think creatively and collaboratively. "We see gaps in three areas," said Moorthy. "One is the ability to apply concepts that have been learned: making that link between the concept and the application. Second is in understanding the impact of teamwork and being able to produce an outcome based on team effort. Third is in the area of communications. We see that all three of these are critical for the knowledge industries. And in the knowledge area itself, while there is one aspect of making the link between concept and application, the depth to which the concepts are covered also varies significantly depending on institutions."

The payoffs for Infosys are enormous. Entry-level employees walk into the organization with all the skills they need to make an impact from day one, and are form-fitted to the company culture. Retention rates are high, and performance issues are low, according to Gurjar. "In spite of being such a large organization, we see very few value-breaks. There are very few deviations from our code of conduct, because, since 60% of our workforce comes from campus, they start believing that this is the way people do business. There is no other way, except the Infy-way, which is [absorbed] into them. That's good for us, and good for our clients, who see very little organizational memory loss because of the strong retention."

All that acculturation may sound a bit totalitarian to Westerners, but the effects of immersive training in creative and critical thinking, business skills, and an understanding of what it takes to serve global markets have a spillover effect that turbo-charges the whole knowledge economy.

"One influence of Infosys has been that it is the hunting ground for any entrepreneur," said Aditya Nath Jha, Head of Global Marketing. "Our people have the skillsets, the experience, the exposure. When startups begin, they want to get a good solid Infosys-disciplined guy, someone who will bring the soul of Infosys [to the new venture]."

Far from discouraging the growth of potential competitors, Infosys embraces its position at the center of India's knowledge economy entrepreneurial ecosystem. "We are a role model for entrepreneurs," said Jha. "This is very important in our context, because traditionally, entrepreneurship in India was limited to a certain group of people like Gujarat or Marwar. They are the business people, they are the traders, and have been entrepreneurs for 5,000 years or whatever. [In the Hindu religion], we have a goddess for wealth and a goddess for studies and education. And they are sisters: Lakshmi and Saraswati. Conventional wisdom in India was that both cannot coexist in the same house. You cannot have education and wealth at the same time, which presumed that education does not lead to wealth. This was pre–knowledge economy. Infosys became a role model [and demonstrated] that through education, middle class boys can become entrepreneurs and make it big. And can do it without compromising on values, ethics, transparency, and integrity. So that's one huge mega umbrella influence that Infosys has had across the country on all fronts."

The second influence was that Infosys created a lot of dollar millionaires through the stock options. This allowed many of them the financial security to go out and take risks, pursue new ideas, and chase their own dreams of leading organizations, often based on the principles they learned at Infosys. "Each one of them hires five more people, so you have many more people going through the startup experience," said Jha.

Finally, Infosys maintains a place within its own culture and organization to nurture entrepreneurs within its ranks.

"We have a program whereby there's a discussion of good ideas [coming from within the company] and how we fund them," explained Gurjar. "And the funding need not just be in money, but in saying that if you're going and starting out a training college, for instance, then is there some way that Infosys can train people, or supports them [in other ways.] So we do a couple of things. We ask, 'Can we help you if you're going out and starting a business?' Two is, sometimes we actually fund some of the entrepreneur ideas."

"One of the things we measure is how much of our revenues come from services that have been created in the last year, three years, five years," said Jha. "We're always on the lookout for good ideas for business within our existing framework. And then we let them run with it. So we bootstrap them and then they run it on business terms."

No one I asked was able to precisely measure the systemic influence of Infosys in India or the world in pure dollar terms, but here's a quick and dirty calculation. According to NASSCOM, the total IT–BPO (Business Process Outsourcing) industry in 2008 was estimated at $71.7 billion, or 5.8% of India's GDP, with software and services revenue at about $60 billion.[25] The total worldwide spend for these services (from India and elsewhere) exceeded $1.6 trillion in 2007.[26] Anyone care to hazard a guess as to what it was pre-Infosys?

As with all of the organizations profiled in this chapter, the story is less about the success of Infosys itself and more about the dynamic it represents. What began as the dream of a few ambitious software programmers in Bangalore in the early 1980s has grown into an industry that has galvanized a country of more than a billion, running on nothing more than human talent. Infosys showed that Lakshmi and Saraswati—wealth and knowledge—could live harmoniously under one roof, and now they've gone walkabout around the globe.

Few if any of the organizations that Infosys has inspired will rise to its heights, but more and more will emerge as regional and global players. The worldwide Net Generation has seized on the power of knowledge, networks, and entrepreneurship to make its impact felt through the creation of innovative, inspiring, and disruptive organizations. In the next chapter, we will examine how this challenges old paradigms and forces the embrace of new strategies to engage the rising Young World.

CHAPTER 4

ENGAGING THE YOUNG WORLD

Strategies for Success

The subjects interviewed in the previous chapter were selected not only for the creativity and innovation of their ventures, but also for their insights. They are more than incidental entrepreneurs; they are vanguards of an emerging global community, keenly aware of their transformative potential and the disruptive power of the Net Generation as a global force. To borrow a term coined by my colleague Daniel Rasmus, they are "ambassadors of the future"—the very specific future of *Young World Rising*—and the commonalities in their approaches and experiences have a lot to teach today's organizations in terms of how to adapt to the conditions that will prevail if that future materializes.

This chapter codifies the lessons from Young World entrepreneurs as they apply to businesses, non-governmental organizations (NGOs) and governments looking for ways to harness the dynamics of the next phase of globalization. This is critical to any organization's strategic planning efforts, because the new multipolar, bottom–up mode of growth implied by the rise of the Young World complements, and in some ways threatens to disrupt, the more centralized model of globalization driven by multinational corporations, world trade bodies, and governments of Organization for Economic Co-operation and Development countries that currently prevails. It presents opportunities to solve many important problems facing the Old World and Young World alike, including issues of the aging workforce, new market growth, sustainability, transparency, and so on. It also poses some serious challenges, especially to incumbent organizations and established high-wage labor markets.

From the depths of the recession that began in 2008 and is only just showing signs of ending as of this writing, it is tempting to see the challenges inherent in this scenario much more clearly than the opportunities. Multinationals don't welcome more competition in their industries and markets; they are trying to protect what they have. The open, cosmopolitan values implicit in the rise of a multipolar world deeply discomfit traditionalists of all stripes, be they religious fundamentalists, nationalists, luddites, or protectionists—and these groups are ascendant in times of economic uncertainty. And I'm sure more than a few readers came away from the earlier sections of this book wondering, "What about my job?"

These are, I'd argue, short term concerns, but important ones insofar as everything that happens in the long run has to make it through the short run first. One foundational premise of this scenario is that the global economy will eventually resume its growth, if not its pre-crisis structure, perhaps as a direct result of the wealth-creating and market-developing activities of Young World knowledge-economy entrepreneurs. The return of opportunity will take the political edge off many of the anxieties of engagement and provide breathing room for the adoption of new models and new thinking.

Obviously, the resumption of growth is an uncertainty, vigorously contested in some quarters for very good reasons. If we remain stuck in a zero-sum, recessionary mode indefinitely, then all bets are off and the fate of the world on many fronts can appear grim indeed. The risks and warning signs are enumerated at the end of this chapter.

I don't discount those possibilities, but the contrarian in me obliges me to explore the less-traveled road of optimism, particularly in this moment of crisis. This is a set of guidelines to consider if you accept the possibility of rebound and expansion, when engagement between incumbent organizations and Young World insurgents will not only be desirable, but essential. By listening to these ambassadors of the future, organizations can formulate strategies that look beyond short-term zero-sum outcomes and toward the win–win scenarios that combine sustainability and prosperity, people and profits.

ENGAGING YOUNG WORLD TALENT

The talent and creativity of *people* power the knowledge economy. For knowledge-based businesses anywhere in the world, engaging with young talent—through direct employment, contingent/freelance work, or outsourcing—is critical to maintaining business continuity and avoiding value breaks.

As we've seen, institutional and grassroots investments in capacity-building are creating a global army of young talent with the raw know-how and, increasingly, the sophisticated polish of business skills, to participate in the knowledge economy at the highest levels. At the same time, North America, Europe, and Japan will start to feel the effects of their aging populations in earnest over the next 10–15 years.

It may seem like the Old World problem (impending workforce shrinkage) and the Young World solution (increasing numbers of skilled knowledge workers) match up nicely. For example, the 47 million additional working age people in India by 2020 just about equals the projected labor shortfall in the rest of the world.[1] But it's not that simple. To effectively engage Young World talent, incumbent organizations need to think about reaching further back into the skills and education pipeline to ensure that capacity scales up to meet anticipated demand; about how to successfully compete for that talent; and about how to adapt organizational workstyles and culture to make the most of the skills that these new faces bring to the workplace.

Co-Create a Talent Pipeline

Capacity-building efforts across the Young World are showing results, and technologies like e-learning show promise in helping greater numbers of young people develop knowledge-economy skills, but the task ahead is massive. Billions of young people are poorly served by the existing educational systems in their countries, and the lack of skills threatens to permanently constrain their future prospects. Turning this around requires an adjustment on the part of employers accustomed to countries that produce a ready-made supply of new knowledge workers who require only a small gloss of orientation to begin contributing at a high level. Not every organization has the resources to participate directly in the education system or to drive change the way that, for example, the Bill and Melinda Gates Foundation can. Still, new organizations and new platforms provide ways for employers to get involved in education earlier, to identify and develop new talent in ways that are specifically relevant to a job, industry or skill-set. Here are some specific strategies suggested by the practices of Young World entrepreneurs, both social and commercial:

Partner with Local Institutions to Build Knowledge-Economy Capacity. Local groups have the expertise to reach their audience better than outsiders, and have a keener eye for picking out promising but underserved groups and individuals. Partnering with local organizations to provide knowledge, equipment, mentoring, internships, and other material support raises achievement potential and aspirations and positions your organization to tap into new sources of young talent. Microsoft's engagement with education-based NGOs is one model; PIN's willingness to partner with public and private entities in a range of creative ways is the same idea reflected from the bottom up.

Invest in Employability, Not Only in Raw Skills. The theme of employability came through loud and clear as a primary area of focus for capacity-building groups, from the smallest to the largest. Mentoring, on-the-job-training, and opportunities for local young people to broaden their horizons contributes to employability. This option is not restricted only to well-resourced firms like Infosys; even small local businesses such as Syntactics can incorporate a formal training and development program into their for-profit operations.

Tap into Talent Networks. The spread of social networking technology makes it easier to engage Young World populations from afar and reach them much earlier in the recruitment process. Creating connections between established employers and the Young World knowledge workforce is a major focus of entrepreneurial innovation. If there is not already a specialized channel for your industry or your organization, consider partnering with a provider to develop one.

Engage Expatriate Communities. The ties between expatriate communities and home countries are strengthening as a result of low-cost communication and the rapid spread of networks. Engaging the local expatriate community provides a ready-made point of entry to tap into the growing Young World talent market, especially as expatriates start returning home to cultivate opportunities.

Look Beyond the Top Tier. Education—especially in IT and engineering skills—is a booming industry across the Young World, and the pool of talent is gradually expanding beyond the narrow confines of the elite schools and major cities. Globals' Suhas Gopinath, for example, was particularly passionate about his company's strategy of looking beyond the shiny credentials of top-tier graduates to find young talent with greater potential and greater ambition. These recruits may need additional investment in basic skills and employability, but many entrepreneurs who spoke with me are convinced that those investments will pay off handsomely.

Make Your Organization a Magnet for Young World Talent

Multinational companies used to be able to rely on their prestige and deep pockets to attract highly educated Young World elites with world-class skills. Now, increasing numbers of indigenous enterprises offer comparable pay and amenities, plus powerful intangibles of pride and nationalism. Just consider the example in the previous section of Argentina's Globant successfully hiring away a senior executive from Google—certainly considered a company with strong business prospects and an appealing workplace culture—partly on the promise of being able to participate in a larger story of regional growth and social development. Multinationals and large indigenous enterprises are also competing with the dynamism of working in an entrepreneurial startup, or with the prospect of starting a business oneself, now that the barriers to entry have fallen so low.

In *Generation Blend*, I looked at some of the ways that companies in "old economy" industries could appeal to the next-generation workforce by embracing more networked modes of communication, both in terms of technology and management. These same principles apply in Young World markets. Young people everywhere want the opportunity to use their education and their familiarity with information and communication technology to make an impact. They also want to be inspired by their work.

Nandita Gurjar said that Infosys, consistently the top-ranked employer for college graduates in India, keeps its preferred status despite offering lower starting salaries than competitors because of three important factors. "We thought it would be things like campus and culture," she said with a laugh. "Actually, these are the things that come back [from our surveys]. One is the leadership, which is highly visionary. Two is values: 'You will never make us do things we don't want to do.' And third one is, 'You invest in us.'"

Here are some lessons from the successful Young World firms I interviewed:

Align Commercial and Social Missions. When I raised the question of "corporate citizenship" with Infosys marketing chief Aditya Nath Jha, his eyes narrowed and his lips pursed. "Let me choose my words carefully here," he said. "What is called corporate citizenship, or CSR, corporate social responsibility, is not a practice or a process here. It's a philosophy. It's embedded in everything we do." Of course any marketing executive would try to position their company as inherently responsible, but the evidence indicates that Young World companies— especially ones created by Net Generation knowledge economy entrepreneurs—make special efforts to create alignment between their commercial goals and the social needs of their community. This is not because of some superior virtue that these businesses possess, but because the enterprises have identified actual market mechanisms that make the pursuit of social goals (capacity-building, problem-solving, sustainability, and so on) more profitable than not pursuing them. Surveys of the global Net Generation consistently show that this kind of creative alignment between social and commercial goals is singularly inspiring to talented younger workers, and organizations who can execute on this strategy will be extremely competitive in recruiting even with lower starting salaries.

Promote a Creative, Flexible Workstyle. At Globals headquarters in Bangalore, they dim the lights and play hide and seek. In Argentina, Globant hosts happy hours and social outings for the staff. Ushahidi's Ory Okolloh, mother of a two-year old child who is already auditioning for television commercials, manages her distributed organization from home so she can balance her work and family responsibilities. Around the world, Young World entrepreneurs strive to design a work *experience* rather than a work *process*, recognizing that young employees see fewer boundaries between work and life. These kinds of workplaces are already known as magnets for creative class talent in developed economies, but they are seen as especially innovative departures in places where most highly paid work is still highly structured, and most organizations are still rigidly hierarchical and formal.

Provide Recognition and Opportunities for Leadership. Talented young people aspire to leadership, usually more quickly than their elders think is warranted. Successful Young World organizations have found ways to recognize leadership, both as a matter of management practice and through the adoption of social networking technology that enables community recognition of valued contributors. Ushahidi, for example, is nearly as committed to raising the profile of African IT talent as it is of promoting adoption of its own product. This is true of most of the African companies I spoke to. Globals founder Suhas Gopinath is increasingly eager to redirect the spotlight away from himself and onto the team members who have built the organization out. Companies such as Globant and Ushahidi encourage their employees to distinguish themselves through contributions to collaborative projects undertaken by the open source community, building a reputation for leadership through action.

Rethink Employment Models

While the hunt for talent is becoming more complex, so too is the whole concept of employment. Outsourcing, contingent staffing, freelance work, voluntary communities in the "gift economy" (such as open source software development), flextime, and workforce virtualization are challenging the old "presenteeism" model, in which employees travel to the office five days a week and work a fixed schedule. These new models lack the security of full-time, salaried work, but they offer flexibility, continuous challenge, convenience, and the possibility of work/life balance that young workers say, in survey after survey, that they prefer to hollow promises of job security and employer commitment. Increasing numbers of businesses in North

America and Western Europe have been experimenting with these new modes of employment, not just because they appeal to younger workers, but for their productivity and environmental benefits, and because flexibility in organizational structure can be a competitive advantage in the race for talent.

Build Culture and Practices that Support Workforce Virtualization. Technologies such as broadband connectivity, secure remote access, and collaboration software are necessary to enable workforce virtualization, but technology alone is not sufficient.[2] Remote workers need to internalize the discipline necessary to be productive outside the traditional office environment, and managers need the skills to coordinate teams of people they can't see in face-to-face situations.

The trust and social capital required to make a distributed workplace run properly is scarce even in many developed countries, and forms slowly. "We don't have that discipline now," admitted Nandita Gurjar. Her concerns echoed those of many HR people I spoke with. "Once we get it, I think this will be a great policy to roll out, but today we have no way of tracking productivity, and we don't want [employees] to feel like there is an extra holiday when you work from home." There are also parts of the world, particularly Latin America, where the social environment of the office sits at the core of the work experience, and the conveniences of telecommuting (flexibility, no need to commute, work/life balance) don't register as benefits to either managers or employees.

The distributed workplace and the punctuated workday are nevertheless emerging as important characteristics of the new world of work. The appeal of placeless work is almost irresistible in parts of the world where the impossible traffic and pollution of megacities make commuting a two- to three-hour per day affair, and where some employers simply refuse to hire people who live outside a certain distance perimeter because of the unreliability of transportation. Organizations that can develop the management skills needed to master workforce virtualization will enjoy an enormous advantage in recruitment, retention, and productivity, especially with Net Generation workers who are already fluent in collaboration and mobile communication.

Leverage Networks and Communities to Achieve Project Goals. More employers are turning to independent contractors, contingent staff, freelance, and part-time work arrangements as an alternative to paid staff positions. Communities provide a convenient point of access where knowledge economy companies can rapidly recruit and mobilize teams around specific projects, or temporarily engage expertise they need to accomplish targeted tasks. More and more of these channels are being developed, almost on a daily basis. Sites like Lucian Tarnowski's Brave New Talent are specifically angled toward "social recruitment" and "online internships," which seek out Net Generation prospects where they live and breathe: Facebook and other online social networks. Going forward, these kinds of resources will provide enormous strategic advantage for organizations that need to find and engage talent on whatever basis—just as they provide good venues for talented independent workers to shop their skills to the most attractive clients.

COLLABORATING WITH YOUNG WORLD PARTNERS

Young World knowledge economy businesses, as we have seen, are climbing the value chain to become more than simple providers of low-cost outsourcing services. They are nimble and ingenious innovators, producers of knowledge, and early adopters of new technology, with aspirations to reach the global market. Some will emerge as competitors to established businesses—or already have. In many more cases, however, Young World innovators provide complementary capabilities that can help Old World incumbents achieve their strategic imperatives: Develop new markets, create new products and services to meet emerging needs, and adapt legacy business models to the new requirements of the interconnected world.

The challenge for established firms, accustomed to a global business environment where innovation and sophisticated business practices flow from the center to the edge, is to adapt to a situation where knowledge can originate from anywhere and flow in any direction. The next great idea can come just as easily from the remote mountains of Colombia or the increasingly self-confident community of entrepreneurs in Cape Town, South Africa, as from the knowledge mills of Silicon Valley. Organizations can prepare for this scenario by developing partnering models for a multipolar world, where partners in emerging economies are not simply commodity providers of low-cost services or outlets for prepackaged offerings but equal contributors in a reciprocal business relationship.

Tap Local Market Expertise

In a 2007 report, McKinsey & Company estimated that the Indian middle class consumer market will mushroom from its current size, which they pegged at 50 million, to 538 million in 2025.[3] Business professor Vijay Mahajan sizes the "Africa-two" (second-tier, aspirational middle-class) consumer market at roughly 400 million and growing.[4] Some of the most vibrant economies in Latin America, though hard-hit by the economic crisis of 2008, not only have been growing in aggregate terms, but also have been making progress increasing the buying power at the base of the pyramid.[5] If these markets return to their pre-crisis strength, the influx of new middle class and middle class–aspiring consumers in the Young World can more than offset demographically related declines elsewhere. This shouldn't be news to anyone at this point. Emerging markets have been a core driver of global growth for the last decade, and most multinationals are pursuing market growth strategies of one kind or another.

The problem with Young World markets from a developed-world perspective is that they are risky and complex. The risks are due to higher levels of social and political turmoil, corruption, uneven law enforcement, and uncertain demand. The complexities involve everything from government regulation and market barriers to the existence of multiple spoken languages and dialects. Even well-resourced multinationals have seen their efforts at market penetration fail from time to time because of unexpected issues or misinterpretation of data.

While many multinationals are wary of the considerable risks in the second- and third-tier emerging economies, local entrepreneurs have no choice but to adapt to whatever conditions they experience, because these are their home markets. They are quietly building social capital, reputation, and connections that can prove the difference between success and failure. As 'Gbenga Sesan responded when I asked him about some of the daunting challenges of doing business in Nigeria, "I do not think the problem is stability; this is a market that has operated even in the most unstable times." The costs of doing business in a high-risk environment are already factored into their models, and the best practices that multinationals learn the hard way (if at all) are already well-known to local operators. These organizations are looking for partners and can bring a lot of valuable knowledge to the table.

Even reluctant partners like Herman Chinery-Hesse learned to appreciate the benefits of reciprocity. In the end, his partnership helped both sides, as Microsoft, through the vehicle of theSOFTtribe's "tropically tolerant" solution, was able to displace rival Oracle in a high-profile deployment, and theSOFTtribes found what Chinery-Hesse described as "an appropriate technology platform" on which to base their business software products going forward.

Look for Reciprocal Opportunities in Outsourcing

For the last 15 years, global knowledge economy outsourcing has been about one thing: price. Young World countries are low-wage countries, and developed economies sent work there to be done at a lower cost than was possible from the high-wage domestic professional workforce. Now that many of the most obvious venues for outsourcing have been mobilized and the available pool of skilled labor is almost exhausted, wages are starting to even out, especially at the high end. Networks are giving knowledge-workers the same disembodied transnational mobility that capital has enjoyed for decades.

Something else is happening as well: The first wave of companies that made their money by outsourcing basic business and IT services are looking to climb the value chain to become innovators in their own right. Now it is they who are looking for partners—not necessarily to do the same work for less money, although that is happening too, but to help collaboratively exploit market opportunities that they cannot tackle on their own, for whatever reason. I am a principal in a Seattle-based digital communications firm, MediaPlant LLC. We're not a large or especially well-known company, but in 2007, we started receiving a steady stream of *bona fide* solicitations by IT services companies from India, Pakistan, China, Latin America and elsewhere, looking for established businesses who could represent their services offerings to large customers in North America or collaborate on specific business and technical opportunities. These weren't the usual scammers and spammers, and they weren't just outsourcers trolling for work: These were businesses, often much bigger than ours, looking for partners.

Outsourcing creates relationships that have the potential to extend beyond business process efficiencies and toward collaborative innovation. Organizations that turned to offshore suppliers to handle structured business processes like call centers, transcription, data entry, and so on might find themselves well-positioned with partners who can help them expand their business, not just save money.

Reach Out to Young World "Consumer Entrepreneurs"

The Young World is home to more than four billion people under the age of 20, and the emergence of a middle class in these countries means an enormous opportunity to reach young consumers. Youth are always trendsetters in fashion and culture, but in large swaths of the rising Young World, they are also the ones with the well-paid knowledge-economy jobs, disposable income, and the sophisticated tastes that come as a result of exposure to global information networks.

On one hand, the globalization of media is creating a worldwide market of Net Generation consumers who have more in common with one another, taste-wise, than they do with older members of their own cultures, making them easy pickings for the purveyors of popular global brands. What works in Rome may also work in Rio. However, tech-savvy young people are not only exposed to international content and brands, but also to the whole mindset that goes with consuming content online.

Part of that mindset manifests in the illicit downloading of music, films, and software—already a huge problem in emerging economies—but there's more to it than simple piracy. Young people who grew up surrounded by digital culture consider themselves co-creators (and therefore co-owners) of the brands and content they consume, because the tools of technology make it so easy for them to customize and personalize that content.[6] The more they participate in the collaborative, social media environment of sites like Flickr, YouTube, Facebook, and the millions of communities of interest across the Web, the more they feel entitled to discuss, criticize, remix, mashup, and recontextualize content, regardless of the formalities of trademark or IP law.[7]

Digital content and social networks have given rise to this new class of "consumer entrepreneurs," and the wider spread of access across the Young World means that the phenomenon will spread as well. Brand and IP owners can consider this a threat or an opportunity. Young World consumer-entrepreneurs bring entire new palettes of ideas to the table. The ways they customize content to fit their tastes and cultures are potentially as creative, and inarguably more authentic, then the best ideas of in-house talent. Organizations that can find ways to tune their listening antennas to these frequencies will likely find a wealth of great ideas, plus new platforms to engage a new breed of young customer.

Participate in Global Communities

Online communities can be productive as well as creative. Whereas Old World businesses and pre-digital generations are scrambling to find ways to adapt their existing practices to networked models, Young World companies are networked by default. When they need help getting the word out, finding resources, scaling up, or getting knowledge, they turn first to their online community. If the community they need doesn't exist, they build one. This gives small players the wherewithal to compete with much larger, better-resourced competitors and enables upstarts to come out of nowhere to challenge incumbents purely on the basis of ideas and execution.

There is no surefire strategy for engaging online communities in the same way that you engage traditional consumer markets. It's a dialogue between equals, not a one-way flow of information from the center to the edge. The economics of these communities can also be frustrating to industries accustomed to linear relationships between content, distribution, and revenue: Just ask a newspaper publisher what they think of blogs, Google, and Craigslist.

Under the surface, however, communities have a very complex social structure in which the currency is reputation. Even an adept Young World organization like Ushahidi had to master the etiquette of engaging the open source community in their software development process, and the Twitter-literate entrepreneurs of Thrillophilia walk a very delicate line between engaging potential customers through social media and spamming people with unwanted solicitations. The way to master the discipline of engaging networks is to try it and fail until you get it right.

INVESTING IN YOUNG WORLD OPPORTUNITY

One piece of the Young World entrepreneurship story still lags behind the others: finance. While institutional and grassroots efforts have increased access and built capacity, and the spread of networks has improved access to knowledge and markets, businesses can only get so far on a shoestring. Now a new financial infrastructure is snapping into place to help knowledge economy entrepreneurs gain the resources they need to operate at full capacity. This presents a whole new set of opportunities for investors willing to tolerate the risks present at the frontiers of innovation.

"A corporate angel network has emerged in India," said A.S. Rao, a business professor specializing in innovation and currently an official in the Ministry of Science and Technology for the Government of India. "It started with The Indus Entrepreneur (TIE); they have something like a hundred-person operation acting in the country. They started this active angel network mentoring the youngsters and the startup people, and then educating them about the scale-up. Their entire focus is only on the scale-up."

He said that the growth of venture capital is new in the last five years, and the increasing availability of seed funding has changed the way young entrepreneurs approach the business. "People are asking, 'Is it a scalable business model?' They are working on their elevator pitch, their golf-cart pitch, sharpening their presentation skills."

Sheraan Amod is a 23-year-old entrepreneur from Cape Town, South Africa, whose online business[8] has already won several innovation awards. When we spoke in April, 2009, he was extremely optimistic about the potential of the Western Cape as a new hotbed of African IT entrepreneurship, especially now that money is starting to flow. "In my opinion, there is an ecosystem in Cape Town that is receiving resources very recently—in the last three years, I would say—and excitement is going up exponentially," he told me. "Right now, we still can't be compared to the developed hubs of the world, because they've had the benefit of venture capital around for decades, whereas in South Africa, that's a fairly new thing. Private equity was everyone's understanding of funding for the last few decades. Real early stage venture capital is a fairly new entrant into the South African financing market and it has a long way to go. But what we are seeing is an excitement and an interest despite the recession. Very few people in South Africa and Cape Town in particular are talking about the global recession. They're thinking about growth, they're thinking of opportunities, they're thinking of all the new funders that are crowding our space now, looking to find new entrepreneurs."

At this early stage, the challenge for investors is that Young World markets—particularly those in the second and third tier—lack transparency, which increases risk. Government regulations do not support business development, either because they are too burdensome, too weak, inconsistently enforced, corrupt, or some combination of all of these. Accounting standards vary, although the best companies understand the importance of implementing the tightest controls from the start. Capitalist ideology still carries a stigma in some parts of the world, even as free-market behaviors predominate. Even though the entrepreneurial community itself is serious and sophisticated, its ways of thinking have not fully penetrated the larger society that surrounds it.

"It's a problem of critical mass," said Ghanaian social entrepreneur Bright Simons. "There is a knowledge elite in Ghana who understand information and communications technology (ICT) issues, understand how ICT can change how the country is run, and understand all these things, but they don't have the influence, so they cannot shift the entire culture. And if you can't shift the culture, then the elite is actually not a vanguard: It's a rebel movement. It's a very isolated rebel movement. The most prominent ICT policy establishment person who runs a center in Ghana has very little influence on policy. In India, they don't need to understand the technology to see that it is big money. That they get. In Ghana, it's not bringing in the money yet."

Investors should watch this social dynamic very carefully. All governments pay lip service to the potential of ICT for economic development, but the maturation of these economies into "information societies" occurs when the knowledge elite begins to have a real role in shaping policy. Simons says that any rapprochement will not be the result of mutual understanding, but will take concerted lobbying. "In Ghana, the current president has appointed several young people to important posts in the government," he said. "It should be the job of the ICT elite to get in touch with those people, because they will understand you better than the old establishment. So we can say, 'One of the ways in which you create [prosperity], hold the populist mantle, and advance your political interest, is to say ICT is the way to go. It would be badge of honor. It will help you compete for political position.' It can be done, but it has to be a [deliberate and organized] effort."

Use Entrepreneur Networks as an Early Warning System

It can be very difficult even for informed outsiders to judge the trajectory of growth and change across distance and cultural boundaries. Mass media reflect the interests of their publishers; academic studies can be painfully narrow; private research is expensive and not always reliable. Fortunately, there are millions of authentic, person-to-person conversations about entrepreneurship, innovation, market conditions, and investment opportunities taking place all the time in hundreds of online communities, blogs, and special interest sites.

Social Networks are Gathering-Places for Entrepreneurs. "Almost every young person I know, and that would be [people] under the age of 27, is on Facebook," said Sheraan Amod. "They're interested in the [entrepreneurship] space. So I feel around me that social networking is fairly ubiquitous and people get what we're talking about. Especially young people. In the local blogosphere, which I read regularly as do many of my friends, Cape Town has now been referred to as Silicon Cape."

Facebook and the other general social networks host special interest sites and groups where investors can tap into the flow of conversation. Others, like Gunjan Sinha's SiliconIndia network, are purpose-built environments for the exchange of ideas and the formation of connections—not just between entrepreneurs themselves, but also to the financial community. All provide points of access and sources of information for potential investors.

Blogs are Excellent Sources of Grassroots Information and Insight. When I started doing the research for this book, one of the first places I turned was the blogosphere. Those initial contacts provided a wealth of knowledge and insights from practitioners, many of which were not yet visible to readers of the *Harvard Business Review*. For example, a whole corner of the blogosphere, including Ushahidi co-founder Erik Hersman's influential White African blog and the Uganda-based Appfrica foundation blog,[9] is devoted to the rapidly-unfolding story of ICT innovation and entrepreneurship in Africa. It can also be handy to know who is talking to whom, and which resources are hubs of influence. Blogs link to each other and provide connections to unexpected ideas and challenging perspectives. Sometimes the links themselves provide evidence of relationships and track the spread of knowledge.

Contests and Innovation Expos Shine the Spotlight on New Talent. "Idea competition is very recent in India," said A.S. Rao, who helped jury an innovation contest in India in 2008 that attracted more than 5,000 entries. He said that competitions are now a common part of "Entrepreneur week" and "Technology Week" events hosted around the country. "There is a large number of youngsters, students, who are now getting into this particular idea generation, idea-initiating, putting themselves in a competition for an idea award. This is something which is very positive. These boys and girls, they think differently. Their perspective is different. We feel they probably would be able to fix long-festering problems, because of the technology in their hands; they are the masters of technology. It's all very promising to me."

He's not alone. Everyone is looking for promising new ideas and business plans across the Young World, especially ones in the ICT industry that have the potential for creating wealth without dependencies on infrastructure and natural resources. The Young Americas Business Trust is only one of dozens of public, private, and NGO foundations that sponsor innovation contests, bringing attention to promising young businesses in need of financing, investment, incubation, and market development. Similar contests now take place across Asia, Latin America, and Africa, showcasing ideas and business models that have been developed with very limited resources but are ready to scale up. For example, the Maker Faire in West Africa, held in

September, is an in-person event, but nonattendees can easily follow the program or see highlights via Twitter and blogs.

Nurture Ecosystems of Innovation

In the developed world, entrepreneurs pursue their ideas supported by a framework of physical infrastructure, social capital, sophisticated financial institutions, and an educated workforce—most of which are the result of public investment and a high-functioning legal and political system. Young World environments typically lack those amenities. Startups in the Young World therefore need to look beyond their immediate environment for various kinds of support. As we've seen, entrepreneurs themselves are creating ways to fill the gaps, sometimes in combination with multinational institutions and government. But as demographics and the spread of technology continue to fire a surge of Young World small business creation and entrepreneurship, this is really an opportunity for engagement by the financial community.

Though venture capitalists have been funding startup incubators in mature markets for decades, the idea is still fairly new in emerging economies. Now we're starting to see the creation of new business parks, office spaces, and shared research facilities—not just to serve the traditional functions of giving small businesses room to develop their ideas, but to provide basic physical infrastructure, such as dependable power, high-speed connectivity, and security, which might otherwise be in short supply. John Guerra of Duto described how his company got a leg up working at ParqueSoft,[10] a software and technology incubation serving 12 Colombian cities along the Velle del Cauca corridor. "At ParqueSoft, you have a lot of companies, a lot of people [who] are doing the same thing you are doing, creating their own companies, so that helps a lot to support your process," he explained. "They have a committee that accepts people to enter the park. In this committee, they give you a training process and ask how you will survive in the park, because when you start your company, you don't have the money to support you."

ParqueSoft was founded by a Colombian entrepreneur, Orlando Rincon, in 1999, to provide support for indigenous knowledge-economy businesses in a very deliberate effort to spur social and economic transformation. The facility claims to have launched more than 400 companies since its inception, and aims to develop more than 1,000 by 2012, to "bring over 200 million dollars annually for the region, transforming Colombia in the Latin American Techno-Knowledge Capital."

ParqueSoft is a standalone venture, but similar facilities around the Young World are being run as part of larger corporations (for example, Infosys, as discussed earlier), by governments, by NGOs, and as part of public-private partnerships. Incubators play an important and respected role in the development of regional entrepreneurial ecosystems, and there is still plenty of room at the ground floor for organizations looking for ways to engage.

DEVELOPING YOUNG WORLD MARKETS

Young World knowledge entrepreneurs are helping to develop their local consumer and business-to-business (B2B) markets in several important ways. First, as we've seen, they increase the capacity of existing businesses by providing them with connections to the global information economy—as in the case of Herman Chinery-Hesse's new online marketplace for traditional African crafts, or Thrillophilia's adventure travel portal. They also make local businesses more competitive through software automation: Dozens of textile spinning firms have adopted StarSoft's line-of-business solution. Finally, they improve the systemic performance of markets by improving access to information or delivering transactional capabilities. India's Reliance Mobile, like many telecom carriers and application developers in Young World markets, offers a selection of thousands of mobile applications to support the rural economy, with everything from pricing and logistics information to operations support (automated crop irrigation, power management, and so on).

The increasing penetration of ICT into various aspects of the economy is changing the dynamics of both the business and consumer markets, such that the well-connected segments of Young World markets are behaving more and more like their peers elsewhere in the world. Even more importantly, bottom-of-the-pyramid (BOP) markets are starting to expect more from suppliers as more and more global brands find ways to scale their offerings appropriately to this increasingly important segment. This creates enormous new opportunities for engagement for companies who recognize that disparities in buying power between developed and emerging markets no longer corresponds to disparities in customer sophistication or expectations of value.

University of Texas business professor Vijay Mahajan is a recognized expert on emerging consumer markets and author of two books on the subject: *The 86 Percent Solution*[11] and *Africa Rising*.[12]

"I think the Internet is clearly [increasing expectations and exposure to the global market], but in addition to that, you have the mobile technology, access to satellite TV—all these technologies collectively have created a lot of awareness," said Mahajan when we spoke in May 2009. "There are still cultural differences from place to place in terms of what we buy and how we consume and when we consume, but overall, consumers are consumers. They want the best product at the lowest possible price, so they want value. The young kids especially: Everywhere they are the same. They love clothes, they love music. They are very much aware of the brands also."

Mahajan believes that many of the difficulties that firms from developed economies have in reaching Young World markets are self-created, the product of what he calls the "14 percent mentality" (the percentage of the world's population that lives in high-income countries). "If your perspective is that the average home is 2,400 square feet, then it makes sense to offer promotions like 'buy one, get one free,' because people have space to store inventory." However, he notes that the mindset is far different for a family of five or six living in 400 square feet. "You don't think about stocking something for a month. It's not possible. So that's where it has a major implication on packaging. There's also a major implication on pricing, because many of these people don't have bank accounts. They need to save [for retirement and emergencies] because there is no social security system. They need to support out-of-work family members." That, he says, leads to practical differences in consumer behavior, but not in the kinds of essential values they are looking for in what they buy.

"It is not that they don't understand the brand or the quality," said Mahajan, citing the example of customers who pay extra for single-serving sizes of branded consumer staples like soap and snacks from Unilever and Nestle, rather than generic, locally-produced goods. "It just makes sense to buy when you need it."

Young World knowledge economy entrepreneurs, who have personal firsthand experience with the consumer mores in their local markets, have found ways to apply the same mindset of scalability and sustainability to the delivery of information services. Bright Simons, for example, created an extremely valuable services based on the relatively cheap, ubiquitous, and lightweight SMS feature common on low-end cell phones. Many other Young World mobile developers are following the same strategy, knowing that the more powerful (and expensive) platforms and networks necessary to support richer mobile Internet applications will likely remain out of reach for average Young World customers, at least for a while.

Mahajan said that the discipline necessary to succeed serving the 86 percent (low-income) market gives Young World firms a leg up in competing with better-resourced rivals burdened with the mentality of affluence. "That's why you see the Chinese and the Indian companies that are dominating many of the countries in Africa. The products and services they have developed for their own countries are exactly the products and services these people need in Africa."

Old World multinationals can compete, of course—especially on the strength of their brands—if they can execute with the kind of precision required, and if they can adjust to the pace of change driven by the emergence of knowledge-based businesses and Net Generation consumer behavior.

Recognize the Emergence of More Complex Consumer Culture

My brother-in-law represented a medical equipment manufacturer in India during the early 1990s and had a rather stark assessment of the market conditions: "If you sell an artificial heart that works for $25 and one that doesn't work for $20, the market will go for the $20 model 100% of the time." That impression—that emerging markets are sensitive only to price—dominated the thinking of many multinationals over the past 30 years, and led to lots of missed opportunities.

Innovation Sells. Innovation analyst A.S. Rao related a cautionary anecdote in our conversation. "Twenty years ago, people took a poll in India, asking which is the most dynamic country. After the U.S., most said Japan. No one [had] heard of Korea back then. But the Japanese companies made a mistake. They said India is a low-cost country, they only go with price, so I should give them the cheapest possible thing. Whether it was Sony, Mitsubishi, all the Japanese multinationals other than Suzuki and Honda—these are the two that really understood it—the big consumer companies really misread India. So they came up with a lagging version of their product in India."

The Koreans, he said, took a different approach. "They started with the best in India. They didn't differentiate. As a matter of fact, many of the products the Koreans introduced first in India, then later in the U.S. In [the United States], there is a perception that Korean products are inferior [to Japanese], but in India, Koreans were an unknown entity. So the Koreans sold a better product, a more contemporary product with a better design, and they grabbed the market. Today in the mindspace of Indians, the Koreans are perceived as more innovative than the Japanese. It's not just a perception. It's a fact in India."

Status Drives the Middle Class Market. In the United States, Europe, and Japan, it may be conventional wisdom that electronic gadgets, computers, and mobile phones are sold as creature-comforts for a spoiled professional elite (and their kids). Interestingly, from the perspective of emerging economies, Old World consumers are much more rationally attuned to the features and capabilities of their gadgets, while their own markets are the ones hostage to the fickle drivers of materialism.

"It's all about status," said Bright Simons in a refrain common to many of the African IT professionals I spoke to. "'I've got Internet in the house,' and that's status. 'I've got an iPhone.' That is status. 'I've got a Nokia.' That is status. The use of it, the use itself, that's almost beside the point. People don't brag in terms of what kinds of fancy things they do or how they can hack and change things, except where it has an economic benefit. Then you have the other elites, the small village elites who are happy to just have the goods. But in between that, you don't see a lot of entrepreneurial thinking, where the ability to use it is your status. That has got to change."

Sandeep Amar, a social media entrepreneur and online journalist in Delhi, provided an example from the Indian market. "Consider LCD televisions in India," he said when we spoke in early spring, 2009. "LCDs are a class thing. People say, 'It ought to be in my house.' A lot of people have LCD televisions. And they are HD-ready, full HD, 1080p and stuff like that. But in India, the signal is not there. There is no HD signal, and there's no sign that it's coming. In India, the maximum signal available is 350 lines. So what I'm saying is that they're buying a television for which [they] don't have the signal."

Global Networks are Creating Asymmetrical Transparency. Even as Amar lamented the provincialism of the Indian consumer, he spoke the borderless cosmopolitan language of the global knowledge elite. Our conversation was peppered with (his) apt and precise references to figures from American popular and political culture. Bill Maher, Ron Paul, Van Halen, Steve Jobs, Beyoncé, housing prices in New Jersey and the pros and cons of shopping at Wal-Mart (which has no stores in India) all made cameo appearances in our wide-ranging discussion. "I'm a regular watcher of Bill Maher; I watch Jon Stewart and I know Jon Stewart had this fight with Cramer, the *Mad Money* guy, just because of the Internet. How else would I get it? The sophistication is growing."

This was a common thread across dozens of interviews I conducted, whether in Latin America, Africa, Southeast Asia, or the Indian subcontinent. U.S. (and, increasingly Japanese) popular culture was ubiquitous and well-known, providing U.S. cultural goods—media, fashion, gadgets, content—with unimpeachable coolness and cachet. It's also made a generation of affluent and well-educated young people conversant in American pop and trivia—the building blocks of a creative economy built on the endless recycling of cultural references. How many Americans could name even a few Bollywood stars, Asian pop chart-toppers, or champion-quality cricket players? In the short term, the hegemony of American pop culture is helping to establish Western brands strongly in the minds of Young World consumers. In the long run, I wonder about the implications of a world where the average person knows so much about us, while we know next to nothing about them.

Complex is the New Simple. So far, we've heard compelling arguments that innovation, value, price, status, and pop-culture coolness are the real driving factor behind Young World consumer market growth. In fact, it is actually all these things, in complex and uncertain combination, overlaid on all kinds of additional local, culture-specific drivers. Companies that want to master this environment should start building local competency and local partnerships now.

Localize Your Social Media Strategy

Most developed-world companies that target the youth market have figured out a social media strategy, typically some combination of viral marketing on social networks, rich media content, community engagement, search engine optimization, with an eye towards whatever is the newest, hottest trend. One would think that the increasing penetration of social media across the Young World might make it easy to port those same strategies to various pockets of Net Gen consumers anywhere on the globe, but my conversations indicated that usage patterns and relationships with local content providers vary significantly.

In India, for example, Bollywood (the Hindi-language film industry, the largest in the world) has taken a huge role in the spread of social media, providing content and using social computing aggressively as a way to promote its products.

"All major media have YouTube channels, and there is an amazing amount of everything in India," said Amar. "YouTube in India is really rocking. Advertisers, television companies, all the content owners have taken to YouTube like wildfire. Indian companies have taken to it more positively than Viacom and some of the other [multinational] companies. They have not taken off their videos. Today, if you look for a Rod Stewart video or a Van Halen video, you won't find it on YouTube. You'll find it on MTV.com, but only for U.S. viewers. People like me can't see a Van Halen video anymore. That's the way it's going. But Indian content like news channels, or entertainment channels and all these big banner Bollywood films are showing a lot of snippets, a lot of songs. They want to attract people to the portals. So that's where a huge effort is happening."

In Nigeria, home of the world's third largest film industry, the relationship between old and new media is not so cozy. "At the moment, I think that while the technology community is willing to engage with Nollywood, which is Nigeria's movie industry, the reaction from their side isn't very positive," said 'Gbenga Sesan. "The reason is very simple. The medium that is used to distribute their work illegally is new media. So they are wary when it comes to engaging new media to promote themselves. There are a few Web sites; there are tools that some of them have embraced, but most of them are satisfied with distributing their products through offline CDs for now. What I think is that in the next few years—give it five years—we are going to have a strong synergy, but for now, it's a love lost in terms of relationships between the two. It's not a very encouraging relationship."

The types of content offered on social networks, and their appeal to Young World consumers, also vary regionally, although not with any geographic consistency. Japanese and Korean manga and anime are incredibly popular among Brazilian teen girls—some of whom are also taking up the East Asian innovation of telling long-form stories in a series of Twitter or Facebook updates. Matchmaking and dating by instant messaging are all the rage in China, where companies are looking for ways to attract new female users online. In Vietnam, music draws 250,000 users to VietHipHop,[13] a combination of music, photo, and video sharing along with social networking, or Sàn Nhac,[14] where registrants can sing karaoke online—with others able to listen in—record themselves singing, and create their own music blogs.

The localization of social media to fit Young World tastes is a booming segment for entrepreneurs, whose companies can offer insight, guidance, and partnership opportunities for multinationals looking for the right approach.

PLAN FOR UNCERTAINTY

So far this book has spent nearly 50,000 words talking about the promise and potential of a world driven by bottom-up growth, and making the case that the poles are shifting in this direction. There is, I believe, ample evidence that youth, technology, and market-based solutions are converging in new and interesting ways, which requires some kind of response from policy-makers, the global business community, NGOs, and concerned individuals. The response I've been advocating in this section is engagement—that is, partnership, investment, and encouragement—because I think that the rise of the Young World is ultimately in everyone's interests as we try to find ways to accommodate a global population of as many as 10.5 billion by mid-century.

Not everyone will agree. All future scenarios produce different winners and losers. For the Young World to rise and bring the rest of the world up with it, some established interests will have to move aside to make room at the table, at least temporarily. This will require shareholders, workers, or constituents to make some short-term sacrifices, for which they will undoubtedly have little appetite. Governments, multinational corporations, and centrally-organized NGOs that claim to embrace progress and prosperity, openness and innovation, free markets and meritocracy, will see their values put to the test. It is by no means certain that they will elevate their principles over their self-interest, and continue to support ideas such as (relatively) free trade, free flow of information across networks, tolerance for diversity, and restraint in the use of military force.

If those norms break down, or the world is subjected to a major external shock (epidemic, environmental catastrophe, prolonged economic collapse, or regional war, for example) that forces a return to zero-sum thinking, then the hopes raised by the potential of the Young World will go by the wayside. In that case, the global demographic trends facing a devastated and divided planet could make Malthus look like a raving utopian.

In light of current events, it is more than prudent to plan for a great deal of uncertainty when it comes to Young World prospects, despite the strong evidence and compelling dynamics supporting them. Some of these uncertainties are natural and systemic, but others could result from poor policy choices. A partial list of risk factors includes:

- *Political instability*. The threats of political instability and conflict are especially high, especially on a country-by-country basis, considering that we are talking about parts of the world with a history of turbulence or at the center of long-standing geopolitical disputes.

- *Environmental and resource crises.* If predicted environmental calamities such as global climate change, or resource scarcities for strategic commodities (e.g., peak oil), arrive ahead of schedule, that could immediately turn the global economy into a zero-sum game where conflict, not engagement, is the order of the day. Even the response to environmental issues introduces uncertainties, in that it changes the patterns of demand for strategic resources—many of which are located in Young World countries.
- *Persistent economic downturn.* There's also the risk of protracted economic turbulence. As we've seen, some Young World businesses can capitalize on the downturn, because their lower cost basis is more competitive and their bottom-up wealth-creating activities are in some ways a counterweight to failures at the top. Nevertheless, it's unrealistic to assume a school of small fish can swim against a strong current indefinitely. Poor global economic performance always has the potential to destabilize governments, delay necessary investments in basic services or infrastructure, and perpetuate individual misery. It carries special risk for the nascent ecosystem of Young World entrepreneurs, because it reduces access to credit and discourages the kind of risk-oriented investments that small businesses need to scale up. It diminishes the buying power of customers in established markets, where Young World entrepreneurs hope to sell their goods and services.
- *Revolt of the incumbents.* Even if all the external assumptions turn out to be favorable and Young World entrepreneurship has much more of an impact on global economic development than most people expect, the emergence of this new dynamic force is highly likely to generate strong reactions from interests threatened by a disruption in the status quo. Large businesses, domestic industries, and protected labor markets will almost certainly fight to maintain their privileged positions, advocating for policies that make it more difficult for upstarts to gain access to markets, provide outsourced services, or compete with domestic firms.
- *Intellectual property clampdown.* There is currently a lot of uncertainty around the future of intellectual property law in a global context, and this poses the most present and specific risk to Young

World knowledge economy entrepreneurs. Strong, well-written, reasonable protections could go a long way toward promoting innovation and rewarding developers of content. However, there is enormous risk that large, influential multinational corporations will use negotiations over legitimate intellectual property issues, such as counterfeiting and piracy, to stifle competition or impose draconian penalties that inhibit the fair use and global spread of new ideas.[15]

- *Role of government.* "Government" is considered by many ideologues to be the natural enemy of free-market entrepreneurship. But as we have seen from the examples, 21st-century entrepreneurship creatively engages government in various ways, and creative, activist government policy is sometimes essential to create and sustain a climate where new companies can compete on a level playing field with better-established firms. When assessing the risks posed by governments to Young World entrepreneurship, it is more appropriate to look at the qualitative content and execution of government policies than to make judgments based solely on whether government is "activist" or "laissez-faire." For example, while over-regulation remains a general risk for small business growth, some requirements for labor, environmental, accounting and reporting, and quality assurance give confidence to foreign partners, investors, and consumers—if the regulations are reasonable, transparent, and fairly enforced. In terms of trade and immigration policy, some governments may be tempted into destructive and short-sighted populism of either the left or the right, or, through inaction, leave in place a status quo in which large private interests can quietly strangle competitors in the crib or co-opt them through anti-competitive measures. Strong governments protect markets, not monopolists. In this sense, strong government can be the ally, not the enemy, of the entrepreneur.
- *Misguided aid.* Established NGOs, through institutional momentum, may cling to misguided and counterproductive strategies that perpetuate the dependency of developing economies and crowd out wealth-creating entrepreneurs.
- *Xenophobia and parochialism.* The global knowledge economy is cosmopolitan by definition. It thrives on the mingling of new

ideas, the infusion of new cultural perspectives, and the ability to constantly question and challenge current beliefs. The traditional enemies of modernity—religious zealots, racists, misogynists, militant nationalists, know–nothings, and political movements that blend all of these into a toxic brew of fear-driven reaction—are deeply threatened by the blended, borderless world of knowledge and business. The West saw the manifestation of these frustrations on September 11, 2001, but the fear of cosmopolitanism and the temptations of violence are not limited to Islamic fundamentalists. In many countries, cultural reactionaries have long been politi-cally allied with free-market capitalists in coalition against statists, organized labor, and urban elites. Both sides of that Industrial Age coalition are showing signs of fraying; the center may not hold. The ongoing realignment of social and political forces around the world, not only in emerging economies where traditionalism remains strong, but also in China, Europe, and the United States, is a great source of uncertainty with profound consequences for Young World progress.

- *Zero-sum thinking.* These negative influences are much more likely to prevail if economic growth and employment remain sluggish. The competitive advantages of outsourcing are singu-larly unpersuasive to someone who has just lost their job; great news about new business starts in Uganda probably does not make the front page in Detroit. People with a high level of per-sonal economic insecurity are far more likely to embrace zero-sum ("if you're getting ahead, I'm falling behind") thinking and fall back on exclusionary traditionalist belief systems, and history shows that can lead politics in dangerous directions.
- *Political Pressures.* The problem with an economic model based on talent is that talent is unequally distributed, and so the rewards will be unequally distributed. Inequality, even resulting from a legitimate competition, generates resentment. If the knowledge economy generates too few winners and too many losers with-out showing evidence of broader social benefits, politicians will feel pressure from left-out constituencies to redress that issue, particularly if the winners flaunt their gains. Even in fast-grow-ing India, the glittering high-tech sector—and the upwardly mobile creative class it has conjured into being—is still viewed

with suspicion by the 800 million people who remain mired in poverty. Entrepreneurs and knowledge elites walk a fine line between pushing for their economic interests (lower taxes, deregulation) and recognizing that their long-term survival depends on spreading the wealth as well as creating the wealth. Until the experience of prosperity permeates the general population, the future of any Young World "economic miracle" will be subject to review with every national election.

For the Young World to rise, it must navigate through this minefield of challenges. Strategists standing at the crossroads at this moment of peak uncertainty need to factor in all of the possibilities—expansion, stagnation, collapse—as they plan for the futures of their organizations. If the downturn persists, will the world turn inward to tend to domestic priorities, or will societies succumb to the seductive lure of extremist beliefs and violence?

If growth resumes, will it be driven once again from the center out, by the large multinationals that propelled the first stage of globalization (and its discontents)? Or will it come from this emerging force of young, tech-empowered entrepreneurs, with their unusual and disruptive approaches that threaten to realign the world into a more multipolar and dynamic economy?

We'll have to wait and see. If growth remains stagnant, then we are in for a long period of turbulence and uncertainty. But if indigenous entrepreneurship in emerging economies gains traction, creates employment, creates buying power and consumer confidence, it could begin to exert demand pressure on North America, Europe, and Northeast Asia. At that point, we will be in for a very interesting 10–15 years as the imagination, energy, and creativity of the Young World finds its full expression.

CONCLUSION

While I was in India researching this book, I had the opportunity to visit the Dharavi slum in Mumbai, made famous in the 2008 film *Slumdog Millionaire*. By official estimate, more than 1.5 million souls are crammed into the one-square-mile, heart-shaped tract between two railroad lines. Some put the number at more than 2.5 million.

Walking the streets of Dharavi is like touring the end of the world—the kind of place we all might end up if the worst environmental and economic forecasts come true. Homes built from corrugated metal are stacked on top of one another, above a foundation layer of trash, mud, refuse, and sewage. The average family dwelling is 125 square feet. There is one toilet for every 1,500 residents.

It is a squalid place, but not an unproductive one. Dharavi's inhabitants produce nearly $1 billion per year in economic output. The slum is home to tens of thousands of microenterprises in dozens of industries, principally the recycling of plastics and metals, the production of leather, the cooking of baked goods that are sold as snacks throughout Mumbai, and the production of ceramics, courtesy of a community of potters originally from the region of Gujarat. The slum-dwellers engaged in these industries manufacture their own equipment and appear to operate in independent collectives, paid by the piece or the final product rather than by the hour or day.

Dharavi's is entrepreneurship of the grittiest sort—probably not far from 1830s London or 1860s New York. The laborers work long days in cramped, unventilated cubbyholes, use dangerous homemade power tools and toxic chemicals without any protection, burn plastic and old T-shirts to fire their kilns, and dodge trucks and motorcycles that race through narrow alleys overloaded with metal canisters and other hazardous cargo.

People in India tell me Dharavi is one of the best such places, catered to by solicitous politicians and businessmen, and furnished with tax breaks and government services because it is situated on valuable land. It has vitality and social cohesion. People flock to it from desolate rural villages, and, when turned away, end up in conditions even more makeshift and rudimentary, further from the center of town.

The streets of Dharavi are teeming with children. This is the true face of the Young World—the conditions under which many of the 4.2 billion Millennials are starting their lives.

The important question for the future—perhaps the most important issue facing the world—is how many of them will have better choices as their lives progress? The conditions of Dharavi are grim, but not hopeless. They do not evoke pity so much as a desire to encourage the forces for positive change that so obviously exist, even amid the poverty. The group that arranged my visit operates a community center offering English language and computer training for local youth, preparing them for entry-level jobs in the knowledge economy. Even the most menial data entry or call center job, after all, pays wages high enough to lift an entire family out of poverty.

Most can't or won't take this path. But if the door is cracked open just a bit to offer at least the hope that a child born with talent, ambition, and curiosity might have the opportunity to find expression for those traits, who knows what kind of ideas might come walking through that door?

In the end, as *Slumdog Millionaire* so optimistically suggests, will at least some of world's poorest make their millions by knowing the answers?

* * *

Several days later, I found myself in a different India altogether: the modern, air-conditioned offices of Globals, Inc. in the northwestern corner of the high-tech boomtown of Bangalore. I was escorted through a maze of cubicles populated by a multinational assortment of industrious Net Generation knowledge workers—tapping busily on keyboards or conversing, in various languages, into their headsets— and shown into the company's conference room.

Across the table was the company's founder, Suhas Gopinath. We had spoken before, but this was the first time we'd met in person. It is impossible to ignore the fact that he's barely 22 years old, but what strikes one first about this international executive is his poise and presence. Suhas's company isn't successful because he's so young—it's successful because he's so smart.

Our conversation ranged over a variety of topics: the recession, the impact of outsourcing, the problems of doing business with corrupt governments, the importance of training young Indians to understand the different sets of expectations that prevail in places like Germany (one of Globals' biggest markets), and the ways that the business climate for entre- preneurs in India has improved since he started the company in 2001.

At one point, Suhas talked about his recent sabbatical, when he stepped away from day-to-day management and left his company in the hands of his employees for the first time. "There were some screw- ups, of course," he said, "but they handled them."

In an instant, the difference in years, miles, and culture that hung between us in that room evaporated. Anyone who has started their own company anywhere, in any industry, could relate to the pride that radiated from him as he told that story.

Suhas took me into a nearby office and introduced me to Amruta Desai, Globals Vice President for Strategy and Marketing. At age 26, she runs the day-to-day account management and business operations for a multimillion-dollar global enterprise with offices in 12 countries. She started with Globals when she was still an undergraduate, and grew into her current responsibilities while completing her MBA.

"When we hire, we ask 'does this person have the skills that we need?' and do not pay so much attention to their academic perfor- mance," she said, perhaps reflecting her own experience as much as the company's policies. "We have a very high retention rate, because we show a lot of confidence in the people we hire and give them opportunities to learn things about business that they would not see working on some project team in a giant multinational."

She said that Globals now recruits from Europe and North America, seeking out young people who want to experience working in the Indian IT industry and who may be looking someday to start their own businesses. At a time when more than 40% of Americans in their early 20s were having difficulty finding full-time employment, there seems to me worse opportunities than spending a year working with an internationally recognized small enterprise at the epicenter of the Young World knowledge economy.

After lunch, Suhas took me around to show me the cyber café (now closed), where he first launched his Web site development business, and then we went for tea to his family home. His mother, who was exactly as I pictured, keeps the young man humble despite his accomplishments, and disapproves of his celebrity.

To the local press, she said, the rising business star might as well have been a Bollywood heartthrob. "The girls, they would throw themselves at him, send him letters saying 'Oh Suhas, if you don't marry me, I will commit suicide!'"

"It doesn't sound like a bad problem until you have it," added Suhas with a shrug.

Lately the buzz has been dying down, which suits him fine. He said he'd rather focus on doing his work and building his company than accepting awards and honors that are based more on the unusual circumstance of his age than his actual accomplishments.

"To tell you the truth, I am getting a bit burned out with the routine at Globals," said the veteran entrepreneur. "Nine years is a long time, and I think it is time for something else. If you are interested, I can tell you about this new project I am planning . . . a brand new Internet company. I am talking to some people and hope to get it started early next year."

EXECUTIVE SUMMARY

KEY TAKE-AWAYS:

- **Youth, technology and entrepreneurship are reshaping the world**. As information and communications technology (ICT) penetration reaches critical mass around the globe, it drives changes in expectations, workstyles, and organizational models. We've seen this happen in developed countries. Its effects will be even more pronounced in countries where legacy infrastructure is weak and young populations predominate.
- **Next-generation approaches are different from what came before**, and this is most visible in the kinds of organizations young entrepreneurs create. Exposure to global digital culture is changing the way young people see themselves, their potential, and the ways they approach problem-solving, leading to the development of a new breed of entrepreneurs capable of addressing 21st century challenges
- **Globalization unleashes talent without borders**. Talent is the competitive advantage in the global knowledge economy.

Globalization creates opportunities for talented people to prosper, regardless of prior geographic, cultural, or historical limitations.

- **Demographic trends favor today's developing countries**. Networks and ICT can transform large populations from a liability ("more mouths to feed") into an asset ("more talent working together to solve problems"). Poorer countries with large young populations can expect a demographic dividend if they make the right investments in technology infrastructure and workforce development.

- **Demographic trends are really bad for China**. The many arguments for China's emergence as the predominant economic and political force of the 21st century need to be weighed against the unprecedented demographic problems they will start to face in the 2020s and beyond.

- **Engaging and encouraging Young World growth is in the interests of the Old World**. The Old World and the Young World are not necessarily in competition – they each need each other to make sure the human race can survive as we hit the peak planetary population of ~10 billion by mid-century.

- **We need to rethink development strategies in light of tech-driven global entrepreneurship**. Indigenous entrepreneurship is the most promising path to prosperity for developing countries. Aid that supports local markets and local providers may be more effective than direct aid to governments.

- **Networked organizational models are the future**. Top-down and command-and-control style management, whether from governments, non-governmental organizations (NGOs) or private companies, is increasingly inappropriate for solving 21st century problems. Young people raised on networks have better ideas that we should listen to.

- **Old divisions between public and private, social and commercial are blurring**. Government, private corporations, and NGOs all have roles to play, but the key is aligning their interests in practical ways rather than asserting that one sector's agenda is ideologically more legitimate than others.

- **Commercial interests and free markets are helping to advance social and economic progress**. The expansion of networks and communication systems driven by commercial interests (telecoms, software and hardware companies, etc.) provides the best avenue for social and economic development by creating venues for high-value, low-capital entrepreneurship.

- **The new knowledge economy is multi-polar**. Great ideas are coming from everywhere, not just the old centers of capital. We need to readjust our antennas to listen for signals coming from the edges of the global economy, because the talented people there often have the best ideas for solving their own problems (and ours).

SUMMARY OF ENGAGEMENT STRATEGIES

- **Engaging Young World Talent**
  - Co-create a talent pipeline with partners
    - Build capacity by partnering with local institutions
    - Invest in employability, not only in raw skills
    - Tap into talent networks
    - Engage expatriate communities
    - Look beyond the top tier
  - Make your organization a magnet for Young World talent
    - Align commercial and social missions
    - Promote a creative, flexible workstyle
    - Provide recognition and opportunities for leadership
  - Rethink employment models
    - Build culture and practices that support workforce virtualization
    - Leverage networks and communities to achieve project goals
- **Collaborating with Young World Partners**
  - Tap local market expertise
  - Look for reciprocal opportunities in outsourcing
  - Reach out to Young World "consumer entrepreneurs"
  - Participate in global communities
- **Investing in Young World Opportunities**
  - Use entrepreneur networks as an early warning system
    - Social networks are gathering places for entrepreneurs

- Blogs are excellent sources of grass-roots information and insight
- Contests and innovation expos shine the spotlight on new talent
- Nurture ecosystems of innovation
- **Developing Young World Markets**
  - Recognize the emergence of a more complex consumer culture
    - Innovation sells
    - Status drives the middle class market
    - Global networks are creating asymmetrical transparency
    - Complex is the new simple
  - Localize your social media strategy
- **Plan for Uncertainty**

For more information and to continue the conversation, go to YoungWorldRising.com.

DIFFERENCES IN ORGANIZATIONAL MODELS

	Old World Model	Young World Model
Optimum Size/Scale	*Bigger is Better*—consolidation, economies of scale	*Speed Kills*—Distributed, networked, ecosystems of nimble organizations
Management Model	Command and control hierarchy; specialization of expertise	Flexible structure, fewer highly defined roles
Employment Model	Permanent, collocated workforce	Distributed, global workforce with multiple employment models
Competitive Advantages	Proximity to financial and knowledge centers; critical mass of resources within organization; ability to influence market and political systems; investments in systems and processes	Ability to discover and mobilize relationships and resources via networks; ability to learn and innovate rapidly; importance to local economy; no legacy investments to maintain
Organizational Mission	Well-defined roles for commercial business, government, social/NGOs	Organizations that blend and blur across boundaries
Emerging Market Strategy	Low-income groups and countries are clients for aid programs and low-priced, low-quality products	Bottom-of-the-Pyramid markets are discerning consumers, demanding innovation and value
Customer Relationships	Broadcast (one-to-many) marketing, customers are consumers	Customers co-create the brand and participate in innovation
Supply Relationships	Supply chain: Low-cost suppliers feed up to high-value producers	Supply webs and ecosystems: Reciprocal value discovery, partners create opportunity for each other
Social Engagement	Corporate Social Responsibility (CSR) is external to core mission, primarily for PR	Organizational mission blends social and commercial goals
Competing for Talent	Attract talent with compensation packages, prestige of employer, amenities	Attract talent by investing in skills, visionary leadership, social mission
Training and Development	Workforce development and capacity-building are the responsibility of government and NGOs	Businesses are critical partners in capacity-building

APPENDIX A

OLD WORLD DEMOGRAPHICS

The following sections detail the impact of aging on the population distribution and workforce composition of the United States, the EU, Russia, and China.

AMERICA LEVELS OFF

In the United States, workforce demographics are a serious but contained problem. Birthrates returned to Baby Boom-era levels after 1980, leading to a jagged population distribution (see Exhibit A.2) with a large bulge for the Boomers (age 46−64 in 2010), a dip for Generation X (age 30−45), and then a widening out at the bottom for the Millennial generation (age 10−29).

The United States reached replacement-level fertility rates for the first time in two generations in 2008, owing almost entirely to U.S. immigration policies and the fecundity of immigrant populations in the U.S. So after nearly four decades of aging, the U.S. workforce will start to get slightly younger again in the mid-2020s,[1] and the median age of the U.S. population will begin to inch down from its peak of 39.1 starting in the 2030s.[2] This should prove an asset, provided of course that the United States is able to educate and prepare its Millennial and post-Millennial youth to take up the challenges of the mid-21st century. Exhibit A.1 shows the projected population and labor force participation rates in the United States through 2050, reflecting greater balance across the age scale.

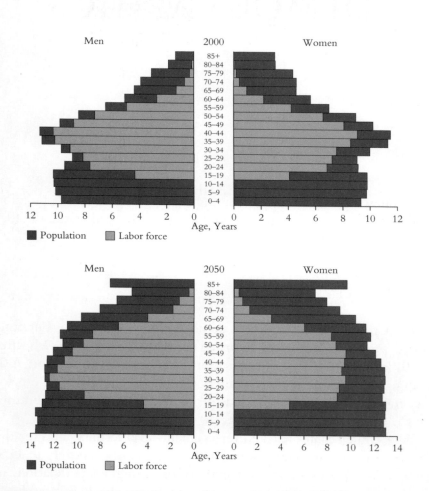

Exhibit A.1 U.S. Population and Workforce Participation, 2000–2050 (projected)

Source: Tossi, Mira. "A New Look at Long-Term Labor Force Projections to 2050." *Monthly Labor Review*, November 2006. www.bls.gov/opub/mlr/2006/11/art3full.pdf

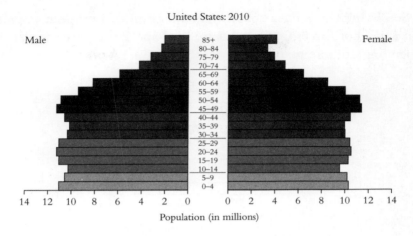

Exhibit A.2 U.S. Population Distribution, 2010
Source: U.S. Census Bureau, 2008.

EUROPE AND JAPAN GO GRAY

Across Europe and northeast Asia, the demographic prognosis is not so encouraging. A generation of European women went through their childbearing years undershooting replacement-level birthrates, leading to a structural reduction in long-term population that will persist even if fertility rates rebound. Whether the young labor force in Europe declines or completely collapses is, in large measure, a function of immigration policies within the European Union, and therefore a great uncertainty.

Conditions vary by country. According to a 2006 white paper on aging populations in Europe:

> The situation of Italy is clearly the worst, due to very low fertility and labour force participation. Ageing processes and their negative labour market consequences are also fairly advanced in Belgium, Bulgaria and Hungary. On the other hand, a relatively good situation with respect to a combination of various support ratios can so far be observed in Denmark, the Netherlands, Switzerland, Portugal, Ireland and the Slovak Republic; in the first four countries mainly due to the high economic activity rates, while in the latter two—to the young population structures.[3]

See Exhibit A.3 for a sobering comparison of European population and labor force distributions in 2002 and 2052 (three scenarios, depending on immigration):

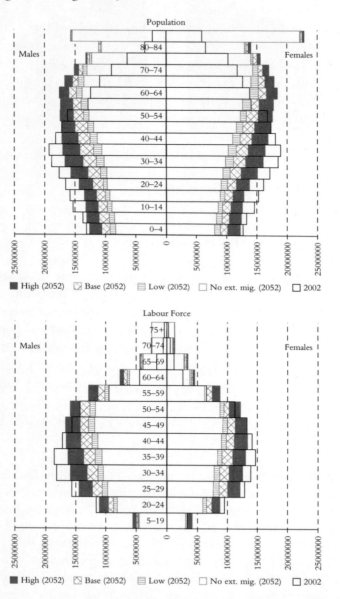

Exhibit A.3 Population and Labor Force Age Pyramids of 27 European Countries, 2002–2052

Source: Tossi, Mira. "A New Look at Long-Term Labor Force Projections to 2050." *Monthly Labor Review*, November 2006. www.bls.gov/opub/mlr/2006/11/art3full.pdf

RUSSIA AND CHINA FACE A DEMOGRAPHIC CRISIS

The scope of this problem is not limited only to the developed world. Russia, Eastern Europe, and China face daunting population and workforce issues of their own, even as they are struggling to emerge as global economic powers.

Russia's population is in steep decline, facing not only diminishing birth rates, but also life expectancies that have fallen dramatically in the post-Communist era to levels well below most of the developed world. Exhibit A.4 shows the impact that these demographic trends will have on Russia from 2002 to 2052.

The former-Communist countries of Eastern Europe have exhibited rapid growth since the 1990s, driven in part by the release of pent-up energies among a population that was better-educated than average and hungry for prosperity. That growth may continue, but it will be driven by increases in productivity (output per person), not demographics. According to a 2008 study by the Transatlantic Council on Migration,[4] the median projection shows the current population of Eastern Europe (about 120 million) shrinking to around 85 million by 2050, on the way toward a reduction of 50% by the end of the century.

China, despite its current success, will soon face one of the most serious demographic challenges in history, as the whiplash effect of the one-child policy and sex-selective reproduction results in the world's largest elderly population, supported by a shriveled workforce of embittered bachelors. See Exhibits A.5 and A.6 to note the dramatic change in the population according to the "medium scenario" projections.

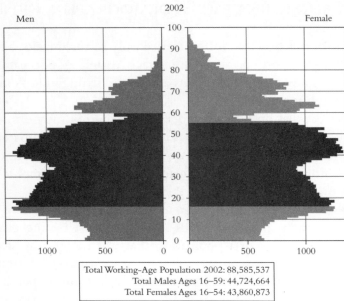

2002

Men   Female

Total Working-Age Population 2002: 88,585,537
Total Males Ages 16–59: 44,724,664
Total Females Ages 16–54: 43,860,873

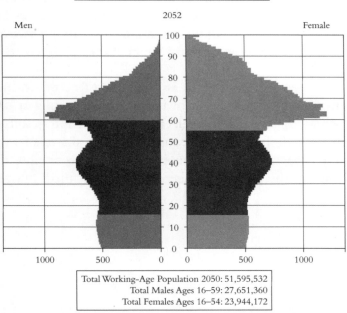

2052

Men   Female

Total Working-Age Population 2050: 51,595,532
Total Males Ages 16–59: 27,651,360
Total Females Ages 16–54: 23,944,172

Exhibit A.4   Working Age Population in Russia, 2002–2052

Source: Donahue, Dennis. "The Future of Work in Russia: Population Projections and the Labor Force."
Presented to the Population Association of America Annual Meeting, April 1–3, 2004, reporting research
and analysis undertaking by the U.S. Census Bureau staff. http://paa2004.princeton.edu/download.
asp?submissionId=41088

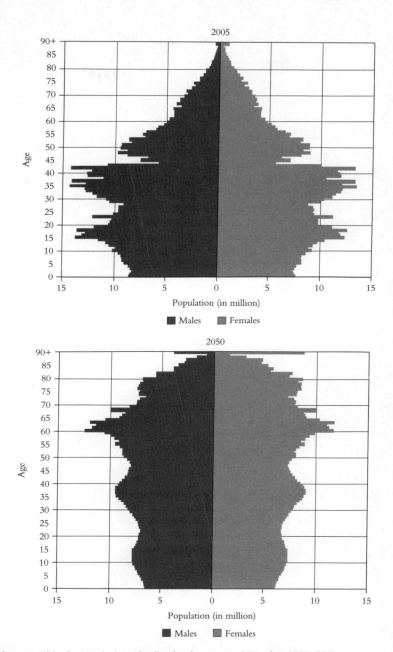

Exhibit A.5 China's Population Distribution by Age and Gender, 2005–2050

Source: Donahue, Dennis. "The Future of Work in Russia: Population Projections and the Labor Force." Presented to the Population Association of America Annual Meeting, April 1–3, 2004, reporting research and analysis undertaking by the U.S. Census Bureau staff. http://paa2004.princeton.edu/download. asp?submissionId=41088, p. 21

APPENDIX B

CLOSING THE DIGITAL DIVIDE

The rise of the Young World depends on the continued spread of technology broadly across the world, and more deeply down the socioeconomic scale. Recent trends show this is happening with increasing velocity, though the gap still remains large in absolute terms.

The speed with which the Young World is closing the connectivity gap is increasing. Sub-Saharan Africa began the decade with one of the lowest access rates in the world—fewer than 0.5 Internet users per 100, below even the 2% average for less developed countries. By 2007, that was up eightfold, to four per hundred—still below average, but with an encouraging rate of increase. Latin America and North Africa/Middle East have seen two of the most dramatic overall increases in both rate and absolute numbers. South Asia has also risen to the developing-country average, with literally millions of users added each quarter. (See Exhibit B.1)

Despite the rapid pace of innovation in this area, gaps still remain. Access and bandwidth in Africa are still, on average, three times the cost of comparable service in Europe and six times the cost of some places in Asia (see Exhibit B.2). For broadband, the gaps are wider. In 2007, a basic DSL (digital subscriber line) package cost an average of $366 a month in

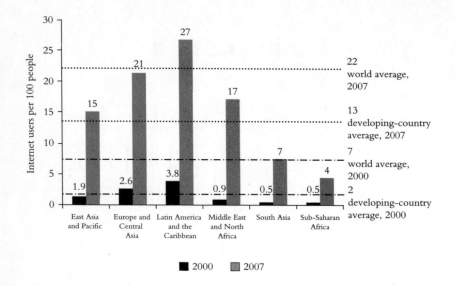

Exhibit B.1 Number of Internet Users by Region, 2000 and 2007

Source: International Telecommunication Union (ITU), World Telecommunications/ICT Indicators Database.

sub-Saharan Africa,[1] compared with $6–$44 in India, while average customers in Organization for Economic Co-operation and Development countries paid only $22 per month for an entry-level package.[2]

The introduction of fiberoptic SAT-3 cables has improved quality of service and availability in Africa, but so far has had limited impact on cost. For example, West Africa is currently connected by fiber to the global network through the SAT-3 cable, but prices for bandwidth are not significantly lower than in East Africa, which did not have fiber backbone connectivity until 2009. The prices of dial-up Internet access in countries connected to SAT-3 remain twice as high as in other developing countries, and operators in South Africa pay eight to ten times more than operators in India for wholesale access to the international gateway.[3] Disparities are wider in rural communities, where it is less profitable for providers to extend service, compared to cities with higher concentrations of more affluent customers and more business activity.

There are signs this may be changing, as demand for affordable bandwidth drives some ingenious business models. In 2009, two Nigerian-born entrepreneurs secured rights to market a suborbital wireless network to be deployed over four countries in West Africa (Sierra Leone, Liberia, Nigeria, and Ghana) using hydrogen-filled weather balloons at an altitude

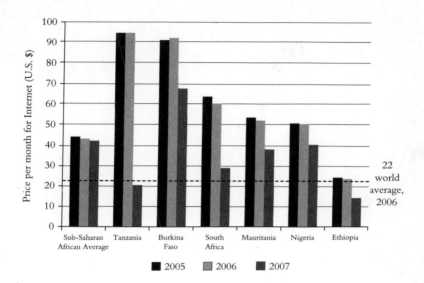

Exhibit B.2 Monthly Price of Internet Services in Various Sub-Saharan African Countries, 2005–2007

Source: International Telecommunication Union (ITU), World Telecommunications/ICT Indicators Database.

of 80,000 to 100,000 feet. The data balloons—which give an interesting new twist to the term "cloud computing"—relay signals from fiber optic cables to tens of thousands of African homes and businesses at speeds from 300 kbits/second up to 10 Mbit.[4]

The long-awaited launch of the SEACOM cable connecting East Africa to India and Europe in July 2009 was greeted with unbridled enthusiasm. "Today is a historic day for Africa and marks the dawn of a new era for communications between the continent and the rest of the world," declared SEACOM CEO Brian Herlihy.[5] The new cable increases bandwidth more than tenfold for customers up and down the eastern edge of the African continent, from Tanzania to Rwanda. "We launched Kung Fu Baby [a YouTube video] and for the first time in Africa, I saw a YouTube video load completely and play in 6 seconds," wrote Kenyan blogger Joshua Goldstein. "We ran a speed test and showed 1.8mbps, 10 times what we have in the Appfrica office."[6] Tanzania's president, Jakaya Kikwete, is only one of several heads of African states who see the opening of the bandwidth frontier as the first step in building an "African Silicon Valley" to serve as a hub for regional knowledge-economy development.

NOTES

INTRODUCTION

1. For a fuller discussion of these themes, see Rasmus, Daniel and Rob Salkowitz, *Listening to the Future: Why It's Everybody's Business*. Hoboken, NJ: John Wiley & Sons, 2009.
2. Zakaria, Fareed. *The Post-American World*. New York: W.W. Norton and Company, 2008, p. 197.
3. Khanna, Tarun. *Billions of Entrepreneurs: How China and India are Reshaping Their Futures and Yours*. Boston: Harvard Business School Press, 2008, p. 22
4. For a fuller discussion of the topic of generational change in the connected workplace, see Salkowitz, Rob, *Generation Blend: Managing Across the Technology Age Gap*. Hoboken, NJ: John Wiley & Sons, 2008.
5. Shirky, Clay. *Here Comes Everybody: The Power of Organizing Without Organizations*. New York: Penguin, 2009.
6. Prahalad, C.K. *The Fortune at the Bottom of the Pyramid: Eradicating Poverty Through Profits*. Philadelphia: Wharton School Publishing, 2004.
7. See Yunis, Mohammed. *Banker to the Poor: Micro-lending and the Battle Against World Poverty*. Public Affairs, 2004.
8. In the formulation of political analyst Fareed Zakaria in *The Post-American World*. New York: W.W. Norton and Company, 2008.

CHAPTER 1

1. Bloom, David and Jeffrey Williamson. "Demographic Transitions and Economic Miracles in Emerging Asia." NBER Working Paper W6268, November 1997. India's demographic dividend is the subject of excellent analysis in Nilekani, Nandan. *Imagining India: The Idea of a Renewed Nation.* New York: Penguin Press, 2009.

2. Wei, Chen and Liu Jinju. "Future Population Trends in China: 2005–2050." Published by Monash University (Australia), September, 2009. www.monash.edu.au/policy/ftp/workpapr/g-191.pdf

3. "World Population Prospects: The 2008 Revision." United Nations Economic and Social Affairs, Population Division, March 2009. www.un.org/esa/population/unpop.htm

4. *The Economist Pocket World in Figures,* 2009.

5. Kenny, Charles. *The Success of Development: Innovation, Ideas and the Global Standard of Living* (Draft). Accessed 6/15/09 from http://charleskenny.blogs.com/weblog/2009/06/the-success-of-development.html

6. "Information and Communications for Development." The World Bank, 2009, pp. 20 and 45

7. Ibid. p. 36

8. Clarke, George, and Scott Wallsten. 2006. "Has the Internet Increased Trade? Evidence from Industrial and Developing Countries." *Economic Inquiry* 44 (3): 465–84.

9. "Information and Communication for Development." The World Bank, 2009, p. 45.

10. Wireless Intelligence, 2008. http://wirelessintelligence.com

11. Quoted in "Should We be Building SMS or Internet Services for Africa?" in White African (blog) by Erik Hersman, August 25, 2009. http://whiteafrican.com/2009/08/25/should-we-be-building-sms-or-internet-services-for-africa/

12. "Approaching the Zettabyte Era." Cisco Systems Whitepaper, June 2008.

13. "General Finding from the Net Gen Global Research Study," New Paradigm Learning Corporation, 2007. Exact figures are Mexico: 405, Brazil: 402, Russia: 412, China: 418, India: 418. The study also surveyed the United States (1021 participants), Canada (815), UK (408), Germany (407), France (411), Spain (408), and Japan (410). This study was designed by Crux Research in close consultation with New Paradigm. The following caveats apply, according to the survey's methodology: "Data were collected via the Harris Interactive Service Bureau using the Harris Poll Online (HPOL) panel of cooperative respondents. Note that by definition an online study cannot represent the Net Generation without Internet access. Internet penetration is high within the N-Gen cohort, but this limitation is important to recognize when interpreting study

results. Similarly, online panels have a tendency to be comprised of a disproportionate number of broadband users, which can affect the response to some questions. Respondents for this survey were selected from among those who have registered to participate in online surveys and polls. The data have been weighted to reflect the demographic composition of online N-Geners. Because the sample is based on those who initially self-selected for participation in a panel, no estimates of sampling error can be calculated. All sample surveys and polls may be subject to multiple sources of error, including but not limited to sampling error, coverage error, error associated with non-response, error associated with question wording and response options, and post-survey weighting and adjustments. Information reported on media use is based on self-reports of online N-Geners. This self-reported data is likely to vary from syndicated audience measurement data."

14. Talpin, John. "Different This Time." TPM Coffee House, June 17, 2009. http://tpmcafe.talkingpointsmemo.com/2009/06/17/different_this_time/
15. Prahalad, C.K. *The Fortune at the Bottom of the Pyramid: Eradicating Poverty Through Profits*. Philadelphia: Wharton School Publishing, 2004.

CHAPTER 2

1. See Dambisa Moyo's challenging critique of foreign aid to Africa, *Dead Aid*. New York: Farrar, Straus and Giroux, 2009.
2. "Gartner Says Emerging Nations Will Make ICT Industry Borderless by 2015—Emerging Markets to Spend Twice the Percentage of GDP on IT Investments Compared to Mature Markets Through 2011." May 14, 2008. www.gartner.com/it/page.jsp?id=669710
3. Nystedt, Dan. "Microsoft Multipoint Livens Thai Math Class." IDG News Service, May 27, 2009. www.pcworld.com/businesscenter/article/165564/microsoft_multipoint_livens_thai_math_class.html For more information on the Multipoint technology, see www.microsoft.com/multipoint/mouse-sdk/
4. See http://download.microsoft.com/download/6/9/f/69f8c76b-198e-4114-9c12-f0b13e4d7e4e/Case%20Study_Morocco.pdf
5. See http://microsoft.com/brazilcs.
6. *IDC Economic Impact Studies for Microsoft 2007*. IDC
7. For more information, see the program's Web site at http://eescola.pt
8. According to Wikipedia, http://en.wikipedia.org/wiki/One_laptop_per_child (Accessed August 10, 2009)
9. For more information about this group, see www.ybiz.net.

CHAPTER 3

1. See my 2008 book, *Generation Blend: Managing Across the Technology Age Gap*, op. cit.
2. Information about the organization can be found at www.pinigeria.org.
3. Information about this organization can be found at www.w-teconline.org.
4. See www.syntacticsinc.com.
5. Rasmus, Daniel W. and Rob Salkowitz. *Listening to the Future: Why It's Everybody's Business*. Hoboken, NJ: John Wiley & Sons, 2008.
6. See the company's Web site at www.bravenewtalent.com.
7. Information about this organization can be found at http://oneyoung-world.com
8. Kiviat, Barbara. "Chasing Desi Dollars," *Time*, July 6, 2005, cited in Kamdar, Mira, *Planet India*. New York: Scribner's, 2007.
9. See www.siliconindia.com/aboutusnew/index.php.
10. Khanna, Tarun. *Billions of Entrepreneurs*. Boston: Harvard Business School Press, 2008, pp. 167–8.
11. "Mobile Phone Users in Ghana Hit 8.7m." Ghana Investment Fund for Telecommunications, June 3, 2008. http://giftel.gov.gh/2008/06/ northern/
12. See www.govloop.org.
13. Okolloh, Ory. "Ushahidi, or 'testimony': Web 2.0 tools for crowdsourcing crisis information." Participatory Learning and Action, Volume 59, Number 1, June 2009, pp. 65–70(6), downloaded from www.ingentaconnect.com/content/iiedpla/pla/2009/00000059/00000001/art00010
14. Ibid.
15. See http://whiteafrican.com.
16. For more information, see the organization's Web site at www.ushahidi.com.
17. See www.ushahidi.com/work, accessed August 27, 2009
18. See the company's Web site at www.thrillophilia.com, or mention on Twitter that you are planning a trip to India and wait for Abhishek or one of his friends to contact you.
19. Chafkin, Max. "Meet the Bill Gates of Ghana." *Inc.*, October 1, 2008. www.inc.com/magazine/20081001/meet-the-bill-gates-of-ghana.html
20. See www.bbc.co.uk/worldservice/specials/1631_judges/page5.shtml.
21. See www.softtribe.com.
22. See www.africabusinesssource.com.
23. See www.globant.com.
24. Sreeharsha, Vinod. "Google's Latin America Chief Jumps to Argentine IT Firm Globant." VentureBeat, April 6, 2009. http://venturebeat.com/2009/04/06/googles-latin-america-chief-jumps-to-argentine-it-firm-globant/accessed September 4, 2009.
25. Strategic Review 2009, Executive Summary. NASSCOM Resource Center. www.nasscom.in/Nasscom/templates/NormalPage.aspx?id=55816.
26. Ibid.

CHAPTER 4

1. Nilekani, Nandan. *Imagining India: The Idea of a Renewed Nation.* New York: Penguin Press, 2009, p. 49.
2. For an excellent discussion of this subject, see Sobel-Lojeski, Karen and Richard P. Riley, *Uniting the Virtual Workforce: Transforming Leadership and Innovation in the Globally Integrated Enterprise.* Hoboken, NJ: John Wiley & Sons, 2008.
3. "The 'Bird of Gold': The Rise of India's Consumer Market." McKinsey & Company Global Institute, May 2007.
4. Mahajan, Vijay with Robert Gunther. *Africa Rising: How 900 Million African Consumers Offer More Than You Think.* Upper Saddle River, NJ: Wharton School Publishing, 2009.
5. For example, see "Brazil as an Equitable Opportunity Society," by Marcelo Neri, in Brainard and Martinez-Diaz, eds., *Brazil as an Economic Superpower? Understanding Brazil's Changing Role in the Global Economy.* Washington, DC: Brookings Institution Press, 2009.
6. For an insightful discussion of this phenomenon, see the forthcoming book on Wiki brands by Sean Moffit and Mike Dover.
7. See Mason, Matt. *The Pirate's Dilemma: How Youth Culture is Reinventing Capitalism.* New York: Free Press, 2008, for a provocative take on this issue.
8. See www.personera.com.
9. See http://appfrica.net, the publishing arm of Appfrica International, a for-profit incubator and software development firm based in Kampala, Uganda.
10. More information is available at www.parquesoft.com.
11. Majahan, Vijay. *The 86 Percent Solution.* New Jersey: Wharton School Publishing, 2006.
12. Mahjan, Vijay. *Africa Rising: How 900 Million African Consumers Offer More Than You Think,* op. cit.
13. See www.viethiphop.com.
14. See www.sannhac.com.
15. In 2009, the controversy centered on the Anti-Counterfeiting Trade Agreement (ACTA), a proposed international convention that seeks to protect intellectual property by requiring network carriers to police the traffic on their networks and restrict access of suspected pirates. Critics are concerned that the lack of due process and the ability of intellectual property owners to insist on draconian penalties against individuals, networks and online services could have a chilling effect on all kinds of online services, including social networks and sites like YouTube, Flickr, and Twitter, where people share content. This could derail the business plans of many legitimate knowledge economy entrepreneurs across the world, including those in the Young World trying to create jobs and opportunities.

APPENDIX A

1. "A Century of Change: The U.S. Labor Force, 1950–2050: With Slower Growth, Aging and Increasing Diversity, the Profile of the U.S. Labor Force is Undergoing a Gradual, but Significant, Change." *Monthly Labor Review*, May, 2002. http://goliath.ecnext.com/coms2/gi_0199-1825587/A-century-of-change-the.html
2. Day, Jennifer. "Population Profile of the United State." U.S. Census Bureau. www.census.gov/population/www/pop-profile/natproj.html
3. Bijak, Jakub, et al. "Population and Labour Force Projections for 27 European Countries, 2002–2052: Impact of International Migration on Population Ageing." European Journal of Population (2007) 23:1–31, p. 5. www.springerlink.com/content/g4727430201744pw/fulltext.pdf
4. Lutz, Wolfgang, Warren Sanderson, Sergei Scherbov and Samir K.C. 2008. Demographic and Human Capital Trends in Eastern Europe and Sub-Saharan Africa. Washington, DC: Migration Policy Institute.

APPENDIX B

1. See www.csiro.au/news/BroadbandNetworks.html
2. "Information and Communication for Development." The World Bank, 2009, p. 51.
3. Neto, I., Niang, C., and Ampah, M. (2005). Fostering pro-competitive regional connectivity in sub-Saharan Africa. Mimeo, The World Bank.
4. Nason, Deborah. "Weather Balloons to Serve Up Web Access in Africa." *Internet Evolution*, June 17, 2009. www.internetevolution.com/author.asp?section_id=694&doc_id=178131&
5. "SEACOM Connects East Africa with the World." *Africa News*, July 23, 2009. www.africanews.com/site/Africa_High_speed_internet_ goes_live/list_messages/26116
6. Goldstein, Joshua. "Kung Fu Baby and the Seacom Cable Launch," posted at *In an African Minute*, July 23, 2009. http://inanafricanminute.blogspot.com/2009/07/kung-fu-baby-and-seacom-cable-launch.html

ACKNOWLEDGEMENTS

It would not have been possible to attempt, let alone complete, a work as ambitious and broadly themed as *Young World Rising* without the insights of the many entrepreneurs, experts, and professionals around the world who were so generous with their time when I came calling.

First thanks are due as always to my colleague, mentor, editor, and friend Daniel W. Rasmus. The work we've done over the years, reflected in our collaboration on *Listening to the Future*, helped shape my methods and inform my research, and our friendship is a continuing source of inspiration.

In 2008, after the publication of *Generation Blend*, I was honored to be invited to join the faculty of nGenera, the Toronto-based research firm founded by Don Tapscott, the world's foremost thinker on the subject of next-generation workforce and collaboration. Thanks to Don, Mike Dover, Paul Artiuch, and the team at nGenera for their collegial support and for sharing the results of their Global NetGen research, which helped frame the discussion in Chapter 1.

Part of my interest in entrepreneurship comes from my own background as an entrepreneur in the communications and media industry.

Thanks to my partners at MediaPlant, LLC in Seattle, Guy Roadruck and Tracey Peyton, plus team members Chris Munson, Miguel Mitchell, Paul Thompson, and Karen Olson. Special kudos to my colleague Janinne Brunyee and my invaluable researcher, Willem Heesbeen, for their contributions to the manuscript.

The book would not have been possible without the generous assistance of the following individuals, who shared their knowledge and expertise or were otherwise helpful in coordinating contacts and resources:

Titi Akinsamni, Sandeep Amar, Sheraan Amod, Pratima Amonkar, Mauricio Cacique Andrade, Fausta Ballesteros, Sonal Bhardwaj, Peter Bowman, Mark Bruening, Stephanie Caragos, Michael Costonis, Lisa Chen, Abhishek Daga, Amruta Desai, Krishna Durbha, Guibert, Englebienne, Matthew Forney, John Alexis Guerra Gómez, Suhas Gopinath, Rui Grilo, Jyotsna Grover, Nandita Gurjar, Santosh Gurlahosur, Chitra Gurnani, Erik Hersman, Herman Chinery-Hesse, Usha Iyer, Joe Jackson, Tarun Khanna, Vijay Mahajan, Unmesh Makyar, Larry Marion, Joshua Marsh, Miha Mazzini, Kalpesh Mehta, Yeruti Mendez, Suhail Mistry, Vaseem Mohammed, Mashka Moomin, Tan Moorthy, Sasha Muench, Anirvan Mukherjee, Wainaina Mungai, Shaliendra Rao Nalige, Aditya Nath Jha, Alexander Oddoz-Mazet, Ory Okolloh, Lakshmi Pratury, Dr. Genevaldo Perpetuo, Professor A. S. Rao, Venkatesh Rao, Francois Rautenbach, Steve Ressler, 'Gbenga Sesan, Vineeta Shetty, Bright Simons, Gunjan Sinha, Ore Somolu, Babatope Soremi, Juliana Tamashiro, Lucian Tarnowski, Melanie Terbeek, Roy Thomasson, Manish Upadhyay, Vidya Vardhaman, Sharon Ann Varghese, Luis Viguria, Rebecca Wayland, Wanda Weigert.

Special thanks to Dheeraj Prasad for his early encouragement, ongoing support, and great help making introductions.

I'd also like to thank the folks who took the time to review the manuscript prior to publication: Mike Dover, Lawrence Wilkinson, Dan Rasmus, Dr. Thomas Kamber, members of the Barnard College Urban Studies "Digital City" seminar, Rebecca Alexander, Guy Roadruck, Ory Okolloh, Ivan Weiss, David Partikian, Mary Jander, June Arunga, Pat Utomi, Bill Wetzel, and Daniel Pink.

Jan Shanahan was instrumental in coordinating the production process, as was Natasha Andrews-Noel. My editor at Wiley, Tim Burgard, was his usual helpful self. Thanks also to Mark Fortier for taking an interest in this project and providing guidance along the way.

Finally, thanks to my staunchest supporter and most perceptive critic, my wonderful wife Eunice Verstegen.

INDEX